To All You

David Halsey

Di,
   Out of the flames
comes life a-new!
Enjoy the journey!
         Your loving friend!
               Judy

FIRE
UP
YOUR
LIFE!

FIRE

UP

YOUR

LIFE!

**With a Wise Man,
a Mentor and an Angel**

DONNA HARTLEY

Frederick Fell Publishers, Inc.

Fire Up Your Life!

FREDERICK FELL PUBLISHERS, INC.

2131 Hollywood Boulevard
Hollywood, Florida 33020
800-771-3355
e-mail: fellpub@aol.com

Visit our web site at www.fellpub.com

This publication is designed to provide accurate and authoritative information in regard to the subject matter covered. It is sold with the understanding that the publisher is not engaged in rendering legal, accounting, or other professional service. If legal advice or other assistance is required, the services of a competent professional person should be sought. From A Declaration of Principles jointly adopted by a Committee of the American Bar Association and a Committee of Publishers.

Library of Congress Cataloging-in-Publication Data
Hartley, Donna, 1947-
>   Fire Up Your Life! : the inspirational story of a wise man, a mentor, and an angel / Donna Hartley.
>   p. cm.
>   ISBN 0-88391-052-7
>   1. Hartley, Donna, 1947-   2. Spiritual biography--United States
>   3. Aircraft accident victims--United States--Biography. I. Title.
>   BL73.H365 A3   2000
>   291.4'092--dc21
>   [B]   00-041717

10 9 8 7 6 5 4 3 2 1

Interior Design by Vicki Heil

The eyes are the window to the soul.

To Sheba, my loyal Himalayan cat, whose
all-wise blue eyes gave me hope.

To Mariah, my precious daughter, whose
laughing green eyes blessed me with love.

To George, my wise man, mentor and angel,
whose enlightening brown eyes awakened my inner vision.

Acknowledgments

To Joan Roelke, my gifted writer, editor and soul mate. Her relentless dedication and energy kept this book moving forward. I thank her for the long hours spent in George's mystical company, deciphering the truth behind his messages and his learning lessons. Without George and Joan by my side, this book would never have been written.

I thank God for friends (and you know who you are) who, when I wanted to give up, pestered me to keep going because they believed this book would happen. From my heart, my deepest appreciation to you all for your insightful critiquing.

To Linda Northrop, a beautiful blond with a great smile, thank you for years of putting up with me and for running my office. Rest in serenity with the angels.

To my publisher, Don Lessne, who had enough faith in me to lead me to success and to Virginia Wells, my editor. I am forever grateful.

To all my mentors who have guided me in body, mind and spirit.

Table of Contents

Section I

THE CRASH

Section II

THE HEALING

Section III

THE DESTINY

SECTION I

THE CRASH

Love and Accept Yourself

It was March 1, 1978, and I was taking off from Los Angeles on Continental Flight 603, and flying to Honolulu to emcee the Miss Hawaii pageant. In 30 seconds, my life changed forever. I was plunged into paralyzing terror when the unexpected happened on lift-off. At a speed of 167 miles per hour, three tires blew. A powerful jolt slammed my body forward so tight against the seat belt, I felt severed at the waist. Bounced and rocked, surrounded by screeching crash sounds, I heard an ear splitting crack as one wing clipped the tarmac and shattered. My breath jammed in my throat and the bitter taste of terror invaded my mouth. I was going to die.

Pandemonium was everywhere: brittle sounds of the plane's cabin breaking apart, panels popping from the ceiling at crazy angles. I cringed at the sight of loose luggage flying through the air and bouncing off panicked passengers — a darkened movie screen collapsed in a heap.

Flight attendants screamed, "Tighten your seat belts! Tighten your seat belts! Then, someone yelled, "Head between your knees — grab your ankles! Head between your knees — grab your ankles!"

Just before I ducked my head down I glanced terrified out the window. We were racing along the runway toward a fenced-in car lot crammed with cars. My heart pounded in my ears and my body shook violently. Eerie silence plagued the entire cabin and I witnessed the fear of death frozen on the faces around me. I dropped my head down, gripped my ankles and immersed myself in a strange union of dread and anticipation.

I had heard that your life passes before you when you die. My life was such a mess for so long, I didn't want to see it. For over thirty years, I had suppressed a childhood plagued by family alcoholism and violence. At six I was hospitalized for malnutrition, and at sixteen my dream of becoming an Olympic skier was snuffed out when I had heart surgery. In my twenties, I hated my body and battled the ups and downs of diet pills, the shame of bulimia — vomiting, fasting, and binging. The men I loved had rejected me, and my deepening sense of unworthiness kept me on the brink of suicide. Now, at last, my wish would come true. In a matter of seconds, I would be dead.

The aircraft was hurtling off the end of the runway with a load of passengers and a belly filled with lethal fuel, and I suddenly felt better than I had at any other time in my life. An all-encompassing calm had descended upon me. Overcome by a rush of warmth and euphoria, I succumbed to a sensation of profound serenity. Joy and peace — tranquil calm descended over me, shrouding me in white light. At no time in my life had I felt such love. I wondered, is this what it was like to die? Was this the mysterious culminating grace, or just a normal reaction before death? Did my comrades feel insulated from their fate by peace and unconditional love? Did they hear what I perceived to be an inner voice speaking a message in the most obtrusive way?

> "You were given this
> life. What have you done
> with it? You can choose to
> die or you can make
> a difference."

As the plane skidded and bounced, I was forced to question my existence on earth. I heard the screech of metal tearing along the left side of the craft. Crash sounds intensified to a roaring din. Seconds before slamming into the car lot, the plane skidded and ground to a halt. My neck jerked back and my hands flew from my ankles. The aircraft had burst into flames and I was entombed in silence.

I slowly raised my head from between my knees. The left side of the cabin had been destroyed and the right fuselage was slanted upward, as if someone had jacked it up some twenty feet in the air. Flames billowed outside my window. What remained of the left wing was engulfed in smoke and yet I sat suspended in a state of bliss. My shield of light was still with me.

An attendant yelled, "Come to the rear!" Frightened passengers swarmed into the aisle to save themselves. Like a remote-controlled robot, I unbuckled my seat belt and advanced into the crowd. I collided with bodies whose only thought was to escape before the plane exploded and trapped them inside. When I reached the end of the sixth row I spied the exit door, but before I could reach it, the pushing from behind popped me out of line like a gum-ball from a vending machine. I tumbled backwards on the tilted cabin floor, fell head first and slid helplessly on my stomach toward the open exit door and the raging blaze outside.

Heat seared my skin, smoke assaulted my lungs and savage flames engulfed the entire rear exit of the cabin. If this was hell, I wanted out. Fool, I thought, it's too late for you. Prepare yourself for a slow and painful death. Suddenly, when there was nothing more than air to prevent me from falling, I stopped moving. I stared into the wall of flames outside and again heard the calming inner voice.

> "Do you love yourself?...
> Do you have a good relationship
> with your family and friends?...
> Are you living your goals and
> dreams?... If you die today,
> have you left this planet a
> better place for being here?"

I lay sprawled on my stomach, hands stretched out before me, transfixed by a toxic bonfire. Sweat streaming down my face, I sobbed, "No — no — no — and no! Inches from mybody, a burst of red-orange flame seared my skin and left me gasping. Just when I had no more than thirty seconds before melting into death, I knew with incredible certainty I had to stay alive. I screamed, "Please — I want to live!"

At that moment, I took charge of my life. I wanted more time to love and redeem myself, to tear down the deceptive shield I had constructed around me because of my own insecurities and fears. My consciousness cried out, "I don't care if I don't have any money, or if I'm alone; I need a chance to make things right!"

Thick smoke and scorching heat squalled inside the cabin A jolt of fear sliced through me as I stared at the flames. If I wanted to live, I had to walk through fire, and *I did want to live*. I gasped back a surge of nausea and struggled to my feet. Step by agonizing step, I struggled my way through the burning flames until I reached the bathroom door. I leaned against it to support myself, jerking away from the hot metal when it seared my skin. Hordes of people were converging on the exit door ahead of me. Attendants were trying their best to maintain order as, one by one, people vanished through the opening to an unknown fate I clawed forward toward the door and an exit clogged with people. How would I get out? The answer flashed through my mind.

"Ask and it will be given, seek and ye will find, knock and the door will be opened unto you."

"Oh please," I begged. "Please. I'll do anything. I don't want to die. Please let me out." Through a haze of pain, I stared in disbelief at a narrow opening on one side of the door, barely enough space for me to slide through. I squirmed through the gap, crying out when heat seared my stomach. A mass of frightened people crowded in from behind and I screamed at them to stop when my right sandal caught on a hunk of protruding metal. I twisted and turned, trying to free my foot as I was thrust toward the ramp by the press of people. My leg was forced into an impossible position, like trying to perform a split. I feared it would be torn from my body. Tears of pain and frustration stung my eyes. To come so far and find death licking her lips once again was unbearable.

"Please," I cried out, "help me." Miraculously, my sandal ripped free and I was catapulted through the door. Down the ramp I plunged in a desperate contorted dance, but both legs were going with me and I was ecstatic. I hit the ground just as an Asian woman with jet-black hair crawled off the chute on her hands and knees. She cried out for help and disappeared, engulfed by smoke. My left ankle exploded with pain, and my leg crumpled beneath me when I crashed to the tarmac. A hundred daggers stabbed at my spine. I pushed pain from my mind and stared at the burgeoning flames surrounding me. My white light energy had disappeared, but I was infused with strength and purpose.

Rivulets of fuel and flames sparkled in a death dance on the tarmac. Loose asphalt dug into my palms and inflammables soaked my jeans. Ugly black smoke rolled menacingly, and fire shot up from the fuselage. I could ignite instantly. I had come so far, only to face extinction again. I put all my weight on my left leg and heaved myself to my feet. Then, I clamped my hands behind me to support my injured back and, dragging my right foot, hobbled clear of the flames. I turned and stared at the blazing aircraft, unable to comprehend if I was really alive, or if this was another of my plane crash nightmares that had plagued me this last year.

The escape chute I had slid down, my wonderful yellow life raft, was now being devoured by smoke and fire. I knew that was real. As real as knowing I'd been the last person to escape from the rear section. The remaining passengers from my section stood helpless at the doorway, entombed in a cemetery of flame. I desperately wanted them safe on the ground with me, and I watched in horrified silence as the slides at the other exits deflated, or caught on fire.

An elderly couple stood at the exit door of the front section hugging each other and staring down at the twenty-foot drop below. He gripped her arm, they gazed deeply at one another, then leapt from the plane and disappeared into the mixture of flames and white foam enveloping the tarmac. Eyes glued to the spot, I chanted over and over, "Let them be alive."

An eternity later, I saw the man stand, catch his balance and pull his wife from the blaze. Her leg was on fire and his face was burned, yet he dragged her to safety.

Shaking violently, tears blurring my vision, I clamped my hand over my mouth to hold back my screams. The bedlam raged on. Fleets of airport fire trucks roared to the crash, luring more people to leap from the plane in a final effort to save themselves. When they landed half-dead on the tarmac, they were pounded to life by a blast of foam from the fire fighter's hoses

A woman's scream broke me from my trance. She had fallen and was writhing on the tarmac. I limped over to her and bent down to help just as two men drove up in an ambulance and warned me away. My outcry went ignored.Just when I could stand no more, a thundering explosion blasted the middle section of the multimillion dollar giant where the fuel tanks lay. The ground shuddered beneath the surface like a massive earthquake, flames shot up like rockets and black smoke mushroomed above us.

A man jumped from the rear exit and landed on the ground. He was burning alive, screaming and crazed by pain. Even foam from the hoses proved useless. A fireman grabbed him and began flailing at the flames with his heavy gloves. He threw the man to the ground and rolled him over and over. The man's head slumped down, his arms hung limp from his smoldering body, and I knew he teetered on the brink of death. The fireman did what he could to comfort the man. Watching him give so unselfishly to an injured stranger, I felt a rush of love for them both. I asked myself why mortals so often must undergo tragedy to express love.

Fifty feet from the mushrooming smoke and flames, stricken survivors clustered together and clung to a chain-link fence, their faces jelled into expressions of horror. The fire was intense, the heat unbearable. I huddled along with the others, sickened by the stench of jet fuel and the burned flesh of the crash victims. A woman next to me clutched her blistered legs and sobbed in pain. The seriously injured lay on blankets, waiting for treatment from medical crews being rushed to the scene in howling ambulances flashing blood-red stroboscopic lights. I pondered why, in the midst of death and unspeakable anguish, did images of my destiny keep appearing in my subconscious? What did they mean? As the fire raged all around me, I heard the inner voice once again.

"Your assignment is to help people help themselves. You will do that by speaking and also—by writing."

I kept thinking it couldn't be me who would do this. "I can't..."

"And you will have a daughter late in life who will be a leader."

I stood there, strength rippling from my legs. Then, I glanced over my shoulder expecting to discover who owned the clear, strong voice, but no one was there. I checked to see if anyone was staring at me, the disheveled woman talking to herself. Though with all we had gone through, I doubted anyone would have noticed, or judged. I played the message over in my mind.

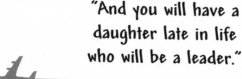

Why did it come to me now of all times? Where did it come from and who sent it? I lifted my eyes to the sky. Could it be?

It was still morning in Los Angeles, but the smoke, ominous clouds and rain had darkened the sky to midnight. A two-car tram from the airline pulled up to transport the ambulatory survivors. Chilled to the bone, smelly, and looking like charred marshmallows, we were wrapped in blankets and helped into the tram. The windows were steamed and the tram's interior reeked of jet fuel from our soaked clothing. Gasping and gagging from the fumes, we pounded on windows and screamed at the driver to let in fresh air. He finally hit the lever and opened the doors. We gulped the smoggy air like it was the purest oxygen.

Bounced like rag-dolls, despair stamped on our faces, we arrived at the Continental Administration Building. A temporary triage center was being set up to provide medical treatment and fresh clothing. I walked into the building dazed and aching. I had an urge to call someone I loved, someone who cared what had just happened to me, someone whose words of reassurance would help glue me back together. I asked one of the volunteers at the triage center where the phones were and she directed me to the Continental Headquarters Conference Room. I was told I could have the room to myself and to call whatever place I wanted and talk as long as I wished. I first spoke with my mother and told her what had happened. She cried hysterically. After I calmed her down, I phoned my brother and then, my father. Each said he was sorry, but they didn't say I love you, or even, I'm glad you're alive. I was hoping for once they could express their feelings and not keep them buried. After I hung up the phone, I folded my arms on the table and stared at the wall. Where was the comfort and reassurance I so desperately needed? Then, I remembered George. Of course — I would call the one friend who was always there for me. A kind man who had entered my life in an uncommon way. Almost as if he were sent to me. When he had predicted certain happenings, I thought he was just weird, but when they came true, we became fast friends. I dialed his number in Oklahoma and was ecstatic when I heard him answer after the first ring.

"George, I'm so glad you're home," I blurted out. "I need to talk to you in the worst way."

"Hey, Partner. What's happened? You don't sound yourself."

"It's me all right." But, not the same me, I thought staring into a mirror on the wall. Fiery red curls lay matted against my scalp, but my full, smooth-skinned face was remarkably composed. My blue-green eyes were plagued by dark circles, but a clarity never there before had emerged. "The outside is not what I would call great, George. I've been injured and burned, but my inside is doing a whole lot better. Remember those nightmares I told you about? The ones about being trapped in a burning plane crash?"

"Of course — sure."

"Well, because of those terrible dreams, I booked my flight to Honolulu four times and guess what? I wound up on the original flight anyway. The nightmares — they came true. I was in a plane crash, George. I almost burned to death." I desperately needed assurance, but got the silent treatment instead. I didn't want to believe George didn't care. "Haven't you got anything to say?"

After a long sigh, he said, "Donna, I do and I understand. I'm just doing some hard thinking. I want to hear more about what happened."

I jumped at the chance. "Okay. You've known me eight years, George, since Hawaii. I thought you were some kind of nut when you insisted we talk — and we've done a lot of that. When I went to Hollywood to become an actress, hit rock bottom and thought about suicide, you said, 'uh-uh, don't do it, Donna. Your life will change in five years — just hang in there.'"

"George, this is the fifth year and I'm thirty years old. Also, why do I have the strange feeling that you came into my life to prepare me for *this* day? " I babbled on. "Because my life was a mess and today, I learned that living is more important than anything."

Images and feelings, welled up in me. Blood pounded through my head just thinking about it. "It was horrible — all those people burning and screaming to get out," I sobbed. "George, I need to find out for myself what caused the accident and who was at fault, because in a mere thirty seconds, life changed for every person on that plane. Why did this happen?"

Choked by emotion I waited, impatient for George to give me answers. I envisioned him standing by the phone, as if we were in the same room together: A calm, forty-something, teddy bear of a man with a kind face and wispy hair combed straight back. Behind horn-rimmed glasses, his clear brown eyes revealed compassion and strength of character. I heard the familiar tap-tapping of his pipe in the background. "George, are you ever going to answer me — or are you just smoking your pipe?"

"I think better with a pipe in my mouth," he eventually said and let loose a long sigh. "I'm sorry you went through this, Donna, but not surprised. It often takes an encounter with disaster to open up a life to something bigger and better than narrow self-interest. You're lucky you learned at such an early stage that the process of shaking things up is what leads us to greater wisdom.

Understand, there is a purpose for everything that happens. Call it, '30 seconds to redemption' or 'a moment of truth'; it's a time when who you are on the inside becomes who you are on the outside."

"That's a lot to learn, George."

"Well, Donna, you're finally getting the big picture — the hard way. A while back I said you first had to learn patience and vision to know what your destiny is. Today earned you the right to discover what the future holds for you."

I wondered if that was what the message meant, my future. I waited out the few seconds of silence while George puffed on his pipe, to hear what kind of direction he would give me this time. We had a pattern. Whenever he spoke his wisdom to me, I always listened first and shot back questions afterwards.

"Today was about transformation, Donna. Your real work is to help other people believe they can have a better life. Through your own experience, you can rekindle their hope."

"George!" I was shocked he knew. "That's what I learned today — I mean — it's what flashed through my mind when the plane crashed and burned — that I have to help people."

He chuckled at the other end of the line. "You know, Donna, there's all kinds of people out there who lack self-esteem, those who choose to exist in the pain they inflict on themselves and others — people afraid to live because they're afraid to fail, so they don't make the conscious choices they need to get them on the right path for what they want. Misery and fear belong to those who like to suffer. Focus, discipline, transformation and, yes, doing some things you don't like to do, open your world to a fresh start. What came to you today was the knowledge that you have the power to help people manifest their own transformation."

I sighed my doubts. "I'm not so sure. Something came to me today, but I think I need to be smarter, deeper and a better person. I don't believe I'm worthy enough to help people."

"Every soul is worthy."

I couldn't believe George had me chatting away when only one hour before, I'd almost died. It seemed odd, but it didn't stop me from talking. "George, my life is a wreck. Besides, with my background, how can I help anybody?" I wailed. "Just for starters, I grew up in a family overrun with alcoholism, violence and divorce. And I didn't exactly graduate at the top of my high-school class. In fact, I couldn't even get accepted to an Ivy League college. I wound up at the University of Montana and after that, the University of Hawaii. They were happy to take anyone because Hawaii had just attained statehood. Oh, and sure, I did win the Miss Hawaii Pageant — after the fifth try. And how many years have I struggled to become an actress? I don't have any money, any career. And you say I can help people?" I hated it when he got quiet. "George, are you smoking again?"

"Just doing a little more brain work. Let me ask you. How does a baby learn to walk?"

"Oh, George, you're talking that Oakie gibberish again." He never seemed to mind my erratic moods, so I in turn answered his questions. "Takes one step, falls down, gets back up, takes another step, falls down. . . What's your point?"

"I'm suggesting you don't need to find an easier life, but one that works. Donna, you've already begun one of the greatest learning periods in your life. The way you have been living is not worth the effort because it does you harm and gives you pain. Right?"

"I won't argue that."

> "Putting forth an effort to make a better life is worth the struggle, because the outcome is a life that serves you.

Consider this, Donna: How did you get out of that plane? Don't answer. I'll tell you. You met your maker and experienced the gift of love and unsurpassed enlightenment. Like a baby taking her first steps, *you walked through those flames.*"

I smiled with remembered pleasure. "George, when I was about to die, I encountered something beyond earthly love, beyond mortal love. It was a feeling of glorious happiness that kept intensifying. I guess I'd call it supreme love. Do you understand what I mean?"

George chuckled the way he did when he got his message across. "Let's just say I've got a pretty good handle on it. And we'll talk more about that when I come to L.A. But, in simple Oklahoma terms, that's what I call a direct hit. The guy upstairs is a great shot."

My throat burned, my injuries throbbed and I wanted to go home. I thanked George for all his wisdom and support and hung up the phone. I limped back to the medical triage where they treated my burns, bandaged my sprained ankle and ordered me home to rest. A Continental employee walked me outside the terminal to the taxi stand. He helped me into the cab and gave the driver a voucher. I wrapped myself in the airline blanket and mumbled my Westwood address to the driver.

He turned his head to speak to me and did a double take. "You okay, lady?"

"Yes," I replied in a listless tone, like I was discussing the weather. "I've just been in a plane crash."

Though my body was burned and bruised and my back throbbed, the sensations that flowed through me during the drive to my apartment were incredibly rejuvenating. I immersed myself in a spectrum of color, texture and sound, and in the skyscrapers and stately buildings I had passed by so often without seeing. The world was so beautiful. I was alive! I gazed at the back of the drivers bald head and smiled. The stranger who protectively wove his cab through traffic wasn't just a stranger driving a beat up taxi, but a fellow being who had hopes and fears just like me. I sensed the healing process had already begun, though

I still had a long way to go. The quiet desperation and sense of abandonment I had wrestled with for so long was reduced to ashes back in the plane crash. George was right. I was spared for a reason. Grateful for my gift of spiritual awakening, I just wondered what lay ahead.

After the cab driver drove away, I limped up the steps to the front door of my apartment. Only when I got inside did I let myself collapse from sheer exhaustion. My first thought was to lie down on the sofa, but then I had an overwhelming desire to fall to my knees and pray. I didn't begin my prayer the usual way, where one gives thanks, though I was thankful, nor did I ask for anything. Usually, the only reason I prayed was when I wanted something, or someone. That's why this moment was so unforgettable. I closed my eyes and shared my most intimate thoughts with God.

"I know you're listening, God. Though we haven't talked a lot, I know you've always been there when I needed you. In the past, I always asked for this and that. Now, I just want to say how much it means to know you loved me and believed in me these past years, even though I had all but abandoned you. After living through the plane crash, I realize now there is a higher purpose and I want to help you do your work. What am I supposed to do? Where do I begin? Please, guide me?"

I kept my eyes closed, my head bowed and waited for a sign or an answer. All during this time I was highly aware that I was not alone in this journey and I would in time have acknowledgment. I don't know how long I remained detached from my surroundings, reflecting in a reverent state. The answer I was seeking was eventually revealed to me in several lifelike situations involving myself and others: on a stage surrounded by a crowd of people, writing in a book, more people; I saw an infant and I perceived it to be a baby girl. After that, I remembered nothing, for I fell into a deep sleep.

When I awoke, I was lying on the floor curled into a fetal position to keep warm. I rolled to my knees, shuddered with pain and somehow got to my feet. I stumbled to my bedroom, dropped my clothes on the floor and collapsed onto the bed. My tremors shook the bed and I pulled the covers tight around me. I had battled death head-on, but I was safe now — safe in my own bed.

At the drifting-off point between sleep and wakefulness, I bolted upright in bed. I mustn't forget what had happened to me. I had to write down my thoughts and the lessons — the entire experience in my own words so I could remember and refer back to it. I turned on the light and removed a pad and pen from the night stand drawer. Later, I would recall how my pen seemed to surpass my thoughts, spiraling down the page at its own rapid pace, and how the extraordinary happenings of that day inspired the birth of my Journal.

JOURNAL
Love and Accept Yourself

Before the plane crash, I was in such pain I had a death wish. I had no acting career and struggled to pay my rent and buy food. I repeated over and over to myself, "*Let my life change. Let it never be the same, or let me die.*"

The four questions I heard in the plane crash altered my thinking and I took action to save my life:

- ❖ **Do you love yourself?**
- ❖ **Do you have a good relationship with your family and friends?**
- ❖ **Are you living your dreams?**
- ❖ **If you die today, have you left this planet a better place for being here?"**

Today I realize how life can take years to change, or it can transform in 30 seconds. Now, I laugh at my blind presumption, because I didn't understand what George meant when he said over and over from the day we met,

> "When you're really sick and tired of being sick and tired, you'll change."

I *was* sick and tired of being sick and tired. For nine days before the crash, I begged for death. From childhood on, I searched for the reason behind the gnawing hunger inside of me. Now I understand why. I did not know love.

I believed returning to Hawaii was my only hope. It was a magical paradise for me, a Shangri-la to heal the soul. I thought if I could go back to the past, I could find love, or it could find me. But, I actually awakened to real love when I chose life over death in the fiery horror of a plane crash. I discovered there was a higher power who loved me for who I was. By understanding death, I understood the importance of life. I learned everyone has to die a little to learn to live. It was when I began to love myself.

And yet, I still have doubt. Today, I love myself, but will I still love myself when I mess up? Why didn't I listen to George? I would have structured my life differently and not waited around for Prince Charming to appear and do what I should have done. I lived an illusion of becoming a famous actress and had sabotaged my own success because I didn't believe I was worthy. I also understand my transformation won't be complete until I put my destiny into motion. People don't need to go through a plane crash to learn about life. Though, I realize the plane crash was inevitable for me because I refused to change.

So, from now on, before bed, I promise myself to do two things: First, I know to keep my life moving forward; personal and professional growth is a necessity. The reason my life path goes in different directions is because I haven't established my values and I can't stay focused. *Universe, what are my true values?* Also, when I ask empowering questions, I'll expect an answer. I understand I could be given a lightening bolt of information, or I could receive segments of data over time.

At the end of each day, I'll give thanks. I took my life for granted and never gave it much thought until I almost lost it. Today, I claim the lessons I have learned. They're mine forever and I don't want to repeat them. The life lesson from the plane crash gave me vision and wisdom:

> "There is a higher power in a divine state beyond myself who has bestowed on me the gift of life. I am worthy of love. I love and accept myself."

Focus On Values

Flames and terrified faces converged on me. An injured man yelled for his wife, and a teenaged girl covered her head with her hands and screamed. Two firemen wrapped a wailing woman's burning leg in a blanket and rolled her on the tarmac.

I bolted upright in bed, awakened by the sound of my own screams. My heart pounded and sweat drenched my nightgown. For several seconds, I didn't realize I wasn't in my own bed. Then, I lay back on the pillow as tears flooded my eyes. It seemed every nerve in my body had gone haywire. It was six days after the crash and I had returned to Honolulu to emcee the Miss Hawaii pageant. I still felt a stranger lived in my body. The crash had taken over my life. I wanted to forget, but the nightmares wouldn't let me. My spirit had gone elsewhere, it seemed. Back to the horror of the burning wreck, back to the victims.

I threw back the covers and walked barefoot outside to the lanai. I sat down on a patio chair, closed my eyes, inhaled the salt-scented air and listened to the soothing sound of frothy white-caps washing over sand. Being near water calmed my frazzled nerves and I stayed awake outside by the sea until dawn. Then, I went inside to shower. I dressed in shorts and a T-shirt and spent the remainder of the day on the beach, wading in the restorative water to soothe my swollen ankle. I wanted to be healthy again. I needed to be centered and happy. I wanted out of aftershock limbo and I was counting on Hawaii to help me.

I returned to my room with plenty of time to primp for the pageant. Against the backdrop of a vermillion sun dipping into the horizon, I dressed in my long white gown. Then, I applied body make-up on my arms and throat to cover the red burn blotches from the flames.

The pageant was held in the main ballroom of the Hilton Hawaiian Village. My back ached and I hobbled across the stage on a swollen ankle. When the judges handed me the list of the top five Miss Hawaii finalists, I turned from the microphone and saw the hopes and fears of the contenders reflected on their faces. Then, I opened the envelope and read off the names. Just before I announced the newest successor, my thoughts flashed back to eight years earlier when I took the joyful winner's walk down the ramp. So much had happened since then. I had struggled hard in Hollywood to become an actress, almost ruining my health because of my bouts with bulimia. I waited for someone to make me a lucky break, not understanding I had to create my own breaks. But, that was the past. Today was a new beginning.

After I crowned the ecstatic new Miss Hawaii, I completed my emcee job and walked off the stage amidst tears of joy and defeat. Just as I reached the exit door leading from backstage, I recognized my friend and Hawaii casting agent, Marge.

"Good I found you, Donna," she said, engulfing me in a hug. "I read in the paper you were in Honolulu. I've got a tip on a TV commercial for you tomorrow. Are you available?"

"Sure," I said. I hadn't talked to Marge in a year and I was happy to know she hadn't forgotten me. She explained Kodak was filming a national commercial. As she rattled off the details, I noticed a well-dressed, slender woman standing by the dressing room. She caught my eye and smiled.

After Marge left, the woman walked up to me and said her daughter, Lori, was in the pageant and that she didn't even make the top five. I merely nodded, sensing her disappointment. Then, she went on to say it was still the best experience of her daughter's life.

I asked how that could be. She said her daughter couldn't stop talking about how I had tried four times to win the title of Miss Hawaii and had finally won on the fifth try. I remembered telling the girls the story. After every loss, I swore I would never run again. But I knew that in order to position myself in my acting career I had to win. The year I won the title, I worked with speech coaches, improved my appearance and worked really hard to build my self-esteem. I focused on winning and by my final attempt, I knew I could do it.

The mother thanked me for conducting myself in a way that was fair and supportive to all the girls. "You were their role-model," she said.

I confessed how the plane crash was a real wake-up call for me, but that learning one's lessons doesn't have to come that hard — it's the choices and results that count. I thanked the woman for her candor. Although her daughter lost, she had learned perseverance and gained confidence.

Alone in my hotel room that night, I was afraid to face another barrage of nightmares and stayed awake long past midnight.

I thought about my Journal and the questions I had asked myself. Could I actually love and accept myself? I hadn't the vaguest idea what that meant. Doubt had crept in like a tulle fog and had again clouded my faith. I covered my face with my hands and sobbed, "Please, God — help me — help me."

The next morning I arrived at my commercial appointment — a cattle call of approximately 50 women. I noticed many of them fit my description and my old insecurity reared its head. Refusing to buckle in to my fears, I pushed away the negative thoughts and told myself I was qualified and deserved the part. Then, I flopped down in a chair to wait. I was the last person to be interviewed. A tanned, blond actor stood nearby while a man and woman asked me questions about my experience. Then, they turned their backs and put their heads together. I overheard them say, "She won't fit the part." And for the two-hundredth time, I heard the words, "Thank you — we'll call you if we need you."

The same old rejection that had knocked me back so many times before. But, this time I decided I would fight back. I figured I had nothing to loose and said to the burly casting director, "I think you're *not* going to call me. I've studied for years. I'm qualified. Why not hire me?"

He looked annoyed and told me I had read well and my background qualified me, but he wanted someone five years older. I asked what the wardrobe was. The woman tossed me a look that would freeze ice-cubes, inhaled deeply, then paged through the script. When she drawled the commercial called for a muumuu and floppy beach hat, I put firepower behind my words and said, "You put one of those big muumuu's on me with a droopy hat, pull my hair back, do my make-up five years older and I would be *great* for the commercial. Thanks for your time." I spun around and marched away.

On the way out, the blonde actor caught up with me and asked if I was always that gutsy. I laughed and said, "Not until seven days ago."

I had entered that room looking confident and cool. I wavered, but persevered. I refused to take the initial rejection as a personal insult. Instead, I reached way down deep inside for my courage, overcame my fears and took action to move me forward. I had to learn the answers, and to do that I had to ask the questions. Even if the answer was one I didn't want to hear, I had gained the information to fight back. I had a purpose and win or lose, I didn't back down and had stood up for myself. I'd always looked outside myself for acceptance, and when I didn't get it, I was devastated. In spite of what happened, I actually felt pretty good.

The next morning, while in the shower, I heard the telephone ring. I reached for a towel and ran to the phone. It was Marge.

"Hi, Donna, hope I didn't wake you. I'm heading for the mainland and I wanted to reach you before I left."

Tension snaked up my spine. I felt the familiar pang of uneasiness when failure got in my face. "No problem, Marge. I don't sleep well these days. Are you — is this about the Kodak commercial?" I clutched the towel tighter around myself.

"Uh-huh, sure is. Donna, I don't know what you said to those people, but you got the job! And they were dogged determined that it be you and only you. I didn't let on before, but the spokesperson for the commercial is Dick Van Dyke, sweetie."

I was overjoyed when a few days later, we shot a perfect commercial with a terrific crew on Honolulu's North Shore. Van Dyke was a true professional who made each of us feel important to him. The backdrop was palm trees and white sand and I fraternized with bikini clad beach bunnies and surfers. I even had a husband — a TV husband for one day. I was 13 pounds lighter from all the stress after the crash. The irony was my costume — a bright red muumuu with little ocean waves on it and a floppy straw hat to match. I looked like a tank.

I wished George was here in Hawaii. His hours of patient listening and insight had at last struck home. I had finally gained some confidence. To hear that from me would please him. I decided I'd call him.

When he answered I said, "Hey, George, guess what? I finally made it to Hawaii. I'm sitting out on the lanai by the water, admiring a fabulous tropical sunset. So how are things in Oklahoma?"

He sighed and said, "Don't get smart. It's cold as marble here." I heard a match strike in the background and I knew George was lighting his pipe. He inhaled a few puffs and said, "I'm thinking about that volcano drink — the one they bring to you all lit up on fire." He chuckled. "So what's going on in beautiful Hawaii?"

"George, I just finished this great TV shoot today. A commercial with Dick Van Dyke. You remember how I read for tons of parts and never got them — well, maybe one or two.

There was always something wrong with me: Too young, wrong color hair, they want brown eyes and mine are blue-green, too fat. . ." I rambled off my list of trivial judgments.

"Slow it down, Donna. Let me ask, were you thinking you *would not* get the part?"

"Actually, all I could think about was landing the job, George. I knew I was equal to any one of the actresses who were competing with me. After all, I had just survived a plane crash and I figured if my maker thought I was good enough to stay on this planet, I wasn't about to be put off by some casting director."

"Ah-ha. That made the difference," George assured me. "Sounds to me like you got some spunk and fought for the job. Am I right?"

"Yes, you're right." I explained my encounter with the casting director.

"That's great. Those TV people had formed an image of Donna Hartley. Then, you turned around and gave them a whole different way of looking at you. You changed their thinking and got the job."

"Coming from you, it all makes sense. I'm just not sure I understand. George, what exactly did I do to cause them to change their thinking?"

"Self-confidence," George said. "You became the person you wanted to be. Remember what happened in the past when you lost acting parts?"

I shuddered just thinking about it. "Do I have to?"

"I'll do it for you," George said. "Those phone calls to me after you drove home at 80 miles an hour on the Hollywood Freeway. You said you wanted to smack right into the concrete divider strip. Why? Because you compared your success in life by how another person judged you and not what you believed you were capable of. How about those times you ate and ate and then threw-up? You had no confidence, Donna. Every time you lost a part, you blamed yourself."

He was so right. "I hope those days are over."

> "Challenges are the mountains we climb in life, and they're never ever over. What makes the difference is how you handle them. Inspiration and desperation drive you to change. You must learn from your lessons, stop those old patterns and move forward."

"Like my men issues, you mean. I repeat that lesson over and over."

"Yes, like the men. You centered your goals and dreams on what they wanted, not on what you wanted. You got hurt."

It seemed George had a way of picking his moments to take me down another path. I heard him at the other end, puffing away on his pipe, cranking up his approach. I could almost smell the ripe aroma of his cherry tobacco.

Then he said, "When you get the big picture, you make better choices."

"Big picture?" I asked.

"Yup.

> **Attitude is the center of life. It's what determines how far you're going to go."**

I moaned. "George — not the attitude thing again. I'm sick of hearing about it."

"I'll bet you are." I heard him draw a few more exasperating puffs on his pipe before he said, "It's time for another of my little stories."

He started by saying that once upon a time there was a father and his beautiful 16-year-old daughter living in a poor section of England. They decided the only way to keep food on the table was to open up a business together. Well, there were no banks at that time, so the father borrowed money from a greedy money-lender. The father agreed to pay back all the money, with interest, in one year. It was pretty risky, because if he couldn't pay all the money back, he'd be locked up in debtors' prison for the rest of his life.

Well, the father and the daughter worked day and night, but the business failed anyhow. The day before the debt came due, the father went to the moneylender and begged and pleaded for more time, but the moneylender wouldn't budge — until he saw the daughter, looking lovely and as promising as a budding rose. He thought for a while and finally said, "I've got a proposition for you. I'll marry your daughter and cancel the debt."

The daughter was terrified and pretty disgusted. She said, "I could never marry a man as mean as you."

"Well, young lady, I have a proposition for you as well," said the moneylender. "Be here in the courtyard at ten o'clock tomorrow morning. I'll put a black pebble and a white pebble in my money pouch. If you choose the black pebble, the debt is canceled, but you marry me. If you choose the white pebble the debt is canceled and you and your father are free to go."

Needless to say, the daughter agonized over her decision. She loved her father a whole bunch and didn't want to see him go to prison, so she agreed. She got to the courtyard just before ten the next morning, and just in time to see the moneylender put two black pebbles in his pouch. He'd tricked her, you see. She was real scared thinking about what would happen to her father — and herself.

When the moneylender held out his pouch to the daughter, she reached inside and clutched a pebble in her fist. Then, she hid it behind her full skirt and dropped it among all the other pebbles in the courtyard. The moneylender yelled at the poor girl for being so clumsy.

"I'm sorry. It slipped from my hand," she said. "But, why don't you reach into your pouch and see what color pebble is left."

Sure enough, only a black pebble was left. The happy daughter shouted, "That means I must have chosen the white pebble."

The moneylender had no choice but to cancel the debt and the father and daughter were free to go their way.

George was silent for a moment, then he said, "I'd guess the moral of that story is no matter how bleak it seems, those choices are just waiting to be discovered if you make up your mind to search for them. That young girl gave it a lot of thought and came up with another solution. It's all attitude, Donna. Think way back, as far as you can remember, when attitude affected the choices you made."

I sighed. "Okay — okay, just give me a minute, but I don't know what difference it makes. Besides, I hated those times."

"What times?"

"When I was a young kid." I dreaded thinking about it. "In my teens I had so many setbacks — boys, schoolwork, health, you name it. Even my prom date walked out on me. After I missed qualifying for the winter ski Olympics because of my heart operation, I developed a very rotten attitude, but I still had hope. To be honest, George, I had so much conflict in my life, I was always going forward and backwards, so I never went anywhere.

"It got worse when I went to Hollywood. Every ounce of my self-doubt was revealed when I auditioned. I looked good on the outside, but on the inside, I was scared to death. I was on that treadmill for quite a while. In fact, I sabotaged my career. Though, I did have some real hope when I became Miss Hawaii." I hesitated, beginning to comprehend what George was working up to. "I had an attitude problem didn't I? I did all the right things, went to acting class and interviewed, but I had no self-confidence."

"You've got the picture," George said and offered a big smile.

> "The best thing anyone can do for a child is to give her self-esteem."

It empowers her forever. Somehow, you got short-changed. Everything has to match to work," George said. "The plane crash made you look at your life, where you are now, where you want to go and what you need to fix to get there."

"George, I'm more self-assured now than ever, but I'm afraid I'll fall back into that unworthy feeling again."

"That's what you have to conquer — fear.

> Quality of life begins in your mind. Trust your attitude, make worthy choices and take pride in yourself."

"And how will I know the right choices?" I asked in a gush of frankness.

"Keep honest with yourself, Donna. Don't lie to yourself and don't lie to other people. Discover what's most important to you and follow those values. Be positive and you'll move ahead."

"You can't move ahead just by just thinking positive, George."

"Of course you can't. You have to follow up with action, but it's the first step toward getting out of a negative pattern." George paused before he spoke again. "I'm going to ask you to do a little list for me. Are you sitting out on the lanai?"

"Uh-huh. And it's so beautiful, George."

He laughed. "Don't rub it in. Find yourself pen and paper and get to work. Write down the five most important things you want in life. I'm not talking about the physical stuff like cars, houses and diamond engagement rings. I'm thinking love, health, family, security, career, independence, spiritual growth — you know."

"George, today I'm in Hawaii and happy. Why do I need to do this?" Silence from the other end was my answer. He was holding firm. I finally said, "So, is there a special way to write this list?"

He chuckled. "Let me say this, there isn't a wrong way to make the list. At certain times in your life you might have love at the top, other times you might have health, family, or spiritual growth at the top. No matter, those five values determine how you live your life. Some people take on their parent's values. Other times you take on the values of people you pal around with. The most important thing is to make your own list. After you do that list, put it in your order of importance."

"Okay — I'll do it." I began at the top and worked down.

After a while George asked, "Tell me what's on your list."

"Love, health. My back still hurts a lot from the crash and my skin needs healing. Of course, my spiritual growth because I want to help people and have conversations with God, like I do with you, George. I want a career and I want a family. That's five."

"Good. Now let me give you a little parable."

I thought, here comes another one. "George, you're always telling me those boring stories," I said.

"You're female, stubborn, Irish, Native American and a red-head. And you need all the help you can get, " George said.

I cringed. "Okay, let's hear it."

"There was a man whom we'll call Pete. Now Pete had values similar to those on your list. He loved his wife and kids, kept himself in good physical shape and he had a fine spiritual relationship with his maker. He was a hard worker who loved his job, but still managed to have quality time with his family. Now, along came a dynamite professional opportunity that would make him a lot more money, but the traveling would give him way less time with his family. Pete decided to accept the new assignment, but as time went on, all that traveling and time away from his family caused him to resent the job. His relationship with his wife was on the decline, his health was failing from rich foods and he gained a lot of weight. Today, all Pete has left is his career, which was number four on his value list. Not his top priority. Do you get what I'm saying, Donna? When you listen to your heart and live within your values, your life flows steady and easy-like.

> **If you live in conflict with your values, you're on a collision course with life.**

When you get back to Los Angeles, prepare yourself to spend a bunch of time healing. That means plenty of rest, good food, lots of water and no late hours."

"I got the message in your story, George, and I kind of figured you were directing it at me. I know I have to stop my harmful behavior patterns, though it won't be easy." I didn't really want to hear the answer, but I had to ask the question. "So, what do you think my negative patterns are?"

"I kinda' hoped you'd ask that. Donna, you have to keep loving yourself and boosting your confidence. Let's wander back a ways. How many times did you run for Miss Hawaii?"

"You know how many times. I was actually stuck losing."

"I do," George said, "but tell me anyhow because it took you a few years to win. That's a good example of how you gained confidence and conquered what seemed a lost opportunity."

I clenched my teeth and said, "I ran four times and lost. The fifth time, I won."

"After the fourth time, when you thought you were a born loser, what made you take that big leap and decide to run again?"

"I'll never forget. I got determined, got advice from supportive mentors and decided to risk it all. I swore I wouldn't lose and be humiliated again. It was win, or nothing. I remember how I kept telling myself over and over, I *was* Miss Hawaii."

"You changed your attitude to accomplish your value which was. . ?"

"A career. Miss Hawaii would position me as an actress and in TV commercial work."

I checked the clock on the night stand and smiled inwardly. We had talked for over an hour. I never tired of talking to George. This dear man could make such remarkable sense out of my jumbled life. I knew he was busy in his own consulting business, but he always made time for me. George kept certain areas of his life discreet. He was helping other lost souls he said were *assigned* to him. I never questioned what he meant by that because he had come to me in such a unconventional way.

Thinking back over the past months, I said, "I love you, George. I can't help but remember the day we met." I had just left the stage after receiving my crown and George was standing there smoking his pipe and wearing a pink and purple tourist shirt. He didn't look threatening — his face was kind, but it was the scent of his cherry tobacco that brought instant comfort to me. He said, "Congratulations, you deserved to win."

I asked him who he was and why he would say something like that. He told me his name was George and that we had to meet at ten the next morning at the coffee shop on the corner. That's when I thought he was some kind of nut, and I told him so."

But George told me my destiny was to leave Hawaii that next year, and I laughed. Then he predicted my car would be towed, my kitchen's leaky pipes would burst and the third step in my apartment would start to creak. It all happened that day just as he said, and I showed up the next morning eager to meet him for breakfast. I was curious then and I'm still curious now.

I've often questioned those weird happenings. I wonder if he was the wise man in my life, the mentor who gave me insight, or was he really some kind of angel sent to watch over me?

"George, exactly who are you?" I whispered into the phone. I was more than a little curious to hear his answer.

After a long pause, George said, "I'll be in L.A. in May. We'll go to that little diner I like. I'll have my coffee, pancakes and bacon. You'll have your herbal tea and yogurt. I don't understand you health nuts. Maybe you could explain *that* to me sometime . . . "

It was late when I got off the phone, but I felt keyed up and not at all tired. George had done a good job avoiding my question, but that didn't mean I wouldn't ask it again. A full moon glowed with promise and the night was charged with tropical scents and balmy breezes. I went inside to my room, leaving the slider door open to the sound of the surf. I picked up a pen from the desk and took my Journal from my suitcase and began to write:

JOURNAL
Focus on Values

It's wonderful to be back amidst all the splendor of Hawaii, my favorite place of all time. It even landed me a first leading role in a national commercial.

And my forever patient pal, George. Our friendship has evolved into a bond of love. He has become my confidant, healer, and mentor. His knowledge about life is amazing and I have learned so much from him. I'm sure my questions drive him crazy, but if they do, he never stops answering them.

Today he helped me discover what values are and about the need to prioritize and pursue them. I realize values motivate me, give me passion, strength to overcome obstacles and pursue my dreams, and they anchor me. Lord knows, I do need a strong foundation. I now understand how growing up, your parents and friends can help establish values for you. I'm 30 years old, and ready to create a set of values that will work for me today. With a little help from George, I discovered the five values that are important to me: love, health, spiritual growth, career and a family.

In the past, love was my foremost value, but I was doomed from the beginning. The men I chose just wanted a good time. They weren't interested in spiritual growth, a loving relationship, or a family. That's what I wanted. Even as I write, I'm gaining an even greater understanding of what George was telling me today. First love yourself, and to have loving relationships that last, you need shared values. I want to be with a man who is not afraid of closeness, sharing and love. That means more than just traveling together, going to movies, having dinner out, or a good time. Those are activities and not values. If I'm to get healthy and stay healthy, I need to think about good nutrition and to release stress. I truly believe I can create what I want because I know what that is. Financial success and a child would make my life complete.

Every night before bed, I'll make some time for my relationship between God and myself. First, I'll place a question in my subconscious when I'm in a calm state. I'll expect an answer in the form of a feeling, an intuitive flash, or maybe even from a conversation with someone. I've never been much of a brand name person, so I'll address the entire Universe which is uniting God's wisdom. The second thing I'll do is express my thanks for the lessons learned. From this, I'll develop compassion, insight and learn clear vision.

Tonight, my all-important question for the universe is: *What should I do next?* I need guidance to fulfill my real purpose. Today's lesson gave me new insight and I claim it. *Thank you, Universe. Learning values are more important than material wealth.* With my new vision, this is what I claim:

> ## I focus on my values and grow strong and wise from my experiences.

VISION THREE

For My Highest Good

I dashed into my friend Mary Margaret's house in California's San Fernando Valley and made a beeline for the kitchen. I didn't slow down until I came face-to-face with the refrigerator.

"Well — hi, Donna — nice to see you. Whatever you find in there, get some for me too," Mary Margaret said, joining me in her warm, cheerful kitchen. "I'll put the kettle on for tea."

Mary Margaret and I had become fast friends at CBS when we attended acting class together. I had even called her for reassurance on the morning of the plane crash after having another of the same foreboding nightmares. The screams, the fire, the bodies — the accident yet to happen. I gathered up cheese from the fridge and some fresh baked bread and laid it out on the kitchen counter.

Mary Margaret glanced at the food and said, "Uh-uh. Bread and cheese — support food. Something you want to talk about, Donna?"

My mind was gushing like a river of muddy water, reckless and not really clear. "Mary Margaret, I just can't do it."

"Do what?"

I dug into my purse and pulled out an official looking document. "It's only three months since the crash and I got subpoenaed by the National Transportation Safety Board. I have to testify at a hearing about the plane crash. And I can't get out of it either." I thrust the subpoena in front of Mary Margaret. "Read this. It says here I'm going to be grilled by powerful executives from massive companies like Continental Airlines, McDonnell Douglas, Goodyear Tire, Goodrich Tire and Pico Chute Company." I took a deep breath and let it out, then hammered at the subpoena with my finger. "And look here, they even listed the Pilot's Association and the Flight Attendant's Association."

Mary Margaret nodded sympathetically and pointed to a cozy nook bordered by frilly curtains and floral patterned wallpaper. "We should talk about this. Sit down, stuff your face and have some tea."

I crumpled the subpoena back into my purse and flopped down on a chair. "I just can't do it," I wailed to my friend. "I've never experienced a situation of this magnitude before. I'm scared they'll try to confuse me because millions of dollars worth of lawsuits are pending. Believe you me, I have crystal clear recollections of what happened that day. In fact, I remembered everything so clearly, I wrote an absolutely consistent report. . ."

Mary Margaret looked up from buttering two slices of bread, concern raining down on her lovely face. "Donna, it's been only two months since you survived the plane crash that changed your life and you're already complaining."

I sighed. She had guessed right. I *was* bellyaching.

"If you don't testify, Donna, who will?"

"I don't know and I don't care." I sat rigid in my chair avoiding Mary Margaret's piercing stare.

"Oh, yes, you do. You're just scared." She picked up the phone and began dialing. "I know just the person who can fix that. My friend Phyllis — Nurse Phyllis."

A short time later, a stern, athletic looking woman in a starched white uniform arrived at the house. Mary Margaret trailed her into the kitchen.

"Hi, Donna," the woman said, holding out her hand to me, "I'm Phyllis, head nurse in the burn ward at Brotman Medical Center — where they took the burn victims after the plane crash."

When I reached out to shake her hand, pain shot up from my lower spine and I suddenly pulled away. "Pleased to meet you," I said, my hand supporting my back.

She said, "I can see you're in pain and I'm sorry, but I don't believe you realize how fortunate you are. I'm leaving for the hospital right now. Why don't you follow me there."

I had an odd sense of forewarning, or perhaps, apprehension. I couldn't decipher which. I only knew I didn't want to go. My jaws started working in protest, but nothing came out. Mary Margaret handed me my keys and in less time than it took to think up a believable excuse not to go, I found myself following Phyllis's white compact car to the hospital.

Thirty minutes later we were walking along the corridor to Brotman's burn ward. When we reached the entrance to the ward, Phyllis paused to pluck two paper gowns from a stack by the door.

"Here," she said, holding out one of the gowns, "put this on. We have to wear them to protect the patients from infection."

I frowned and did as she asked. Not knowing what to expect, my anxiety level was skyrocketing.

"You'll see patients with disfigurements," she explained impassively. "Not only bodies have been damaged, but lives as well. We keep them on IV drips to replace the loss of fluids. There is so much physical and emotional pain the drugs can't relieve. Some of the victims were brought here with their skin still burning beneath the blankets," Phyllis explained.

I couldn't even imagine. "Do you think they'll ever forget this horror?" I asked.

"That's a tough one to answer, Donna." Phyllis sighed heavily and said, "Forget? No. Heal? That all depends on the person. It takes time for people to pass through the psychological stages of what has happened to them. There's denial, anger, grief, self-pity — and mercifully, acceptance."

I shuddered and remembered the man I'd seen running on the tarmac — a fireman beating out flames from the man's smouldering back. I still suffered recurring flashbacks of human torches jumping off the burning plane and rolling on the ground.

"Time for us to go into the ward," Phyllis said abruptly.

I followed her through the doors to a scene that was far beyond my worst nightmare. Vertigo assaulted my equilibrium. Bile rose up in my throat at the horrible stench. My legs got weak. I gripped a table to balance myself and ward off the telltale signs of a panic attack. Just when I was about to cave in, the panicky feeling diminished. Damp with sweat, I accompanied Phyllis from one bed to another, listening to her greet each patient in a casual, matter-of-fact way.

I saw swollen and deformed human beings, tubes protruding from their bodies and burn wounds crusted over like rare hamburger meat. Several times, I turned away repulsed, and then became embarrassed when I saw Phyllis watching me.

A severely burned woman propped up in bed moaned from across the room. I recognized her as a fellow passenger. She must have remembered me also, for she raised a frail hand and waved me over. I frantically looked at Phyllis for support. She nodded and we walked over to the woman's bedside. Her voice was raspy and I had to lean in close to hear her.

"You were there," she murmured, "Why did this happen?"

I was so choked by emotion, I couldn't speak. I slowly shook my head.

"I don't want this to ever happen again to anyone else," she whispered. "No one should have to live in this much pain." Then, she turned her eyes toward the wall.

I knew I had to do something. But what? I didn't yet understand this moment was to be another turning point in my life. I was suddenly ashamed of my weakness. I fled the room, tearing my paper gown off as I ran. When I reached the corridor, I sagged against the wall, gasping for air. I wanted, with every ounce of my healthy flesh, to do something for the dead and injured who couldn't speak for themselves. I was afraid, but at that very moment, I made up my mind to testify. *If not me, who?*

I felt a hand on my shoulder. I glanced up at Phyllis then lowered my eyes. My actions were unworthy of those suffering people and I could hardly look at her

"Go on home now," she said. "You did good." She slipped back through the doors like an angel in white.

I smiled back tears, grateful she didn't censure me for my wretched behavior. Swallowing back nausea, I ran down the stairs and out to the parking lot, where I fell to my knees like a sick dog and vomited. After I pulled myself together, I stared up at the windows where the ward was located and realized that it could very well be me fighting to get well, or worse, to stay alive.

I dragged myself to my feet and walked slowly to my car. When I unlocked the door, the interior of my blue Mustang was stifling. It didn't seem to matter. All I could feel was the pain of the victims. I turned the key in the ignition and leaned my head against the wheel. If I decided to testify, how would I prepare? Within seconds, the answer came to me. George — of course— I would ask George.

By the time I had reached my apartment and climbed the steps to the second floor, I was exhausted by the responsibility of my decision. Fear had nested in my stomach and I was again feeling vulnerable. The mere idea of a panel of lawyers and authorities asking intimidating questions was very scary. Could I do it? And what if the things I said hindered more than helped? I kept thinking someone else could do a much better job of it. But, I couldn't shake away the heartbreaking images in the burn ward. And my mind wouldn't stop its persistent chanting, *if not you, who?*

The phone rang and rang, but no George. Disappointed, I hung up. I wanted to discuss my decision with him. At age twenty five, George had talked me out of suicide and told me to hang in, because when I was about thirty, it would all change. I assumed he meant a great career, a loving husband, money and a fabulous house. Wrong. Life was changing, but in a way I never expected. I was now personally committed to testify at the hearing and had less than a week to prepare. The unforgettable pain on the faces of the burn victims was responsible for my decision to waive my right to sue the airline. I didn't want to be accused of testifying for any money I might be awarded. If my testimony was to make an impact, I had to focus on helping the injured. I pondered over what kind of advice George would give me. Then, I heard his voice, clear as if he was standing next to me, "Donna, there is a part of you that knows what it should do and a part of you that's afraid.

> **To master conflict, you have to tell the truth."**

I smiled inwardly. *Yes, George. I understand* — or did I? Perhaps I could turn to my journal for a plausible explanation.

I sat on the edge of my bed with the journal on my lap. To continue my writing, I felt the need to assess what I had learned up until now. I slowly turned the pages, stopping when certain phrases caught my eye and fit my state of mind. *Learn to love and accept yourself.* Had I done that? If so, then I am the right person to testify. *I focus on values.* I repeated my values out loud — "love, health, spiritual growth, career and family." But where, I asked myself, did the people in the burn ward fit in? The answer came to me immediately. Of course, love, my number one value. My bond with my fellow passengers would give me the strength and empower me to testify. I understood testifying was not without risk. I could anger people and they might not like me for what I say, but I must overcome my fears.

No matter what all those powerful executives and experts said to try and make me distort the truth, I would tell my story, from my point of view, of what actually happened in that plane. I would relive the plane crash and every sordid detail. As a survivor and a victim, I would explain what safety regulations were missing and which needed to be enforced. I had to be convincing, so they would take me seriously. Though I was unable to converse with George in a normal way, I somehow had the premonition he was with me in spirit, that he had tapped a direct line into my consciousness and had canceled my doubts.

During the days preceding the hearing, I spent hours in the library doing research on the causes behind major plane crashes. I called my pilot and flight attendant friends and bombarded them with questions. I was focused and determined to become a spokesperson for the dead and injured who couldn't speak.

✈ ✈ ✈

The hearing was held at the Hyatt Hotel next to the Los Angeles airport. I walked slowly down the corridor, repeating in rhythm with each step, *I can do it, I'll testify, I'll tell the truth.* Inside the main ballroom where the hearing was being conducted, hundreds of people were seated in the gallery. Men in business suits sat at tables situated in front of the chairman conducting the hearing. I swallowed past the huge lump in my throat, found an empty chair at the very back of the room and sat down. My heart was racing. I took a deep breath and willed myself to remember the victims in the burn ward. *I can do it.*

The chairman's words boomed impressively from the front of the room. "This hearing is now underway — 9:00am — May 30, 1978 — to investigate Continental Flight 603 on March 1, 1978 from Los Angeles to Honolulu. He recited the plane's infractions: tire failures, the aircraft's inability to stop after rejected take-off and the DC-10's inadequate emergency evacuation system. Then, he introduced the technical panel members and delegates seated at tables. *I can do it.*

I listened attentively, reconstructing the event in my mind's eye. I heard how the captain averted an even greater disaster by reacting in 1.7 seconds, way below the normal 4.1 seconds. I silently thanked him. Then, I heard my name called: "Miss Donna Hartley — please step up to the witness stand." I was the first person called to testify. My mind raced through what I would say. *I can do it.* I began to sweat and my heart pounded so hard against my ribs, I actually believed people in the room could hear it. This was my moment of decision. I inhaled deeply, rose from my chair and walked to the witness stand.

"Miss Hartley," I heard, "please tell as precisely as you can what happened to you as a passenger on Flight 603."

I described the crash, then I calmly and truthfully answered a barrage of questions from the panels of experts.

I knew very little about the technical stuff, but I had learned enough to express an opinion. Thinking about the victims had me fired up. I had questions of my own and realized this was the perfect opportunity to speak out. *If not me — who?*

I lifted my head and asked, "Why didn't your slide, or chute, or whatever you call it, hold? Can you tell me what happened?"

From a table in front, a distinguished looking man with a full head of gray hair replied, "Your slide at the rear exit held for approximately 25 to 35 passengers, until the fabric tore away from the aircraft and ignited."

He reinforced what I already knew. The last person to exit from the slide was me. I winced and pushed the memory away. This was my only chance to speak out. "Some of the passengers came out of the cockpit window, narrowly escaping on a rope. Why don't you have a rope at every door like they did in the cockpit? People had to jump twenty or thirty feet to the ground. And I never knew anything about a chute before I was trapped in that plane. Why not show a safety film? TV grabs our attention more than the flight attendants." I noticed two men nodding. They were actually listening to me. "What about more focus on tires? From what I read, the three tires that blew out were re-treads and one was patched."

My comments caused a heated discussion. I soon realized the panel had no clear-cut answers. Finally, after two hours on the witness stand, the man who had sworn me in asked me to step down. When proceedings came to an end, I felt proud. For the first time, I had walked willingly into real conflict, and now I was walking away from it intact. Like George said,

> **"The truth will set you free."**

I kept focused throughout the entire encounter and was rewarded with a special bonus. I learned I could push past my fears.

I walked out of the hearing room and was shocked to see the media waiting. Dozens of microphones were thrust at my face and I answered one question after another. When I could stand no more, I broke away from the reporters and fled outside. I sat down on a bench beneath a shade tree, happy it was over. My back and neck throbbed. I was so caught up in my pain, I didn't notice the young man who sat down next to me.

"Hiya," he said. "I don't mean to intrude on your privacy, but could I ask you a question or two?"

I glanced over at the clean-cut man and recognized him as one of the reporters from outside the hearing room. I didn't feel like talking to anyone, but that didn't seem to stop him from asking his questions.

"So, what's it really like to look death in the eye?" he asked. "Was it scary?"

When I saw he wasn't recording me, I decided he deserved a response, so I smiled and said, "You might think this a strange answer, but it wasn't scary. When I knew I was about to die, I couldn't recall ever being so calm. It took a plane crash and facing death for me to really start living. I got a second chance."

"What's so different now?" he asked.

I recalled George saying,

> "Knowledge isn't worth a hoot unless you pass it on to others."

I said, "A miracle happened. I had what is called a 'white light experience'. I was asked four questions and held accountable. I felt compelled to answer."

"Accountable? What kind of questions?" he asked.

"I'm going to ask you the four questions," I said, "and then you'll be accountable:

❖ **Do you love yourself?**
❖ **Do you have a good relationship with your family
   and friends?**
❖ **Are you living your goals and dreams?**
❖ **If you die today, have you left this planet a better
   place for being here?"**

I left the pondering reporter sitting on the park bench and headed for the parking lot. I was shocked to see George leaning against my car, smoking his pipe.

"Hi partner," he said. Have a busy day?"

"George," I exclaimed, "what are you doing here and how did you find me?"

"The news about the hearing was in all the papers. I figured you could use a friend today."

"You bet I can. George, you won't believe what happened to me. I went to the burn ward, made up my mind to testify at the hearing and then I was scared to death and I almost didn't. . . ."

"Take a breath, Donna." He pointed his pipe at the car door. You drive. Let's go to that little fish restaurant in Venice Beach."

The fish and chip restaurant was a fast, no frills kind of place and always busy. The main menu was fish, french-fries and cole-slaw. While waiting in line we talked about the trial. As always, the Venice boardwalk was swarming with fascinating characters: people gliding by on roller blades, little old ladies in mini-skirts with outrageously dyed purple hair, a tattooed man with a snake around his neck and another man juggling chain saws.

"George turned to me with a bewildered look on his face and said, "Did you see those people? Don't you think that's pretty strange?"

"What?"

"In Oklahoma, we don't have that kind of stuff going on. You Californians come from the other side of the rainbow."

I laughed and said, "George, you are what I would call a conservative man."

After we had sat down at our table and the waitress served our fish and chips, I looked across at George and said, "I have a hundred questions to ask you."

"Can I eat first?"

I smiled. "Heck, no. I can talk and eat. Can't you?"

George rolled his eyes and flung me an exasperated look. "Donna, what do you suppose I did in a past lifetime to deserve you in this lifetime?" I noticed the familiar twinkle in his eyes when he said, "I guess there's no getting around that inquisitive itch of yours, so start talking, but first, pass me the tarter sauce."

Just talking to George had a soothing effect on my raw nerves. I don't know how he did it, but he could always calm me down. I sure did miss him when he wasn't around. "Say, why have you waited so long between visits to California? Where have you been?"

"Well, meeting with the people again. Always meeting with my people. Dallas, Denver and there about," George said between mouthfuls. "Things have a way of going where they're supposed to go. Odd how I got my degree in Engineering and here I am doing — consulting. But, I get a chance to wear my engineering hat when I meet with my inventor clients and we discuss their ideas. It excites me when I see new discoveries coming out to help people."

"George, I always hear you say you want to help people. I hardly ever hear you say anything about yourself. It's always about someone you helped or someone you want to help."

He didn't speak for several minutes and I noticed a rare look of sadness had come into his eyes.

"It gets lonely when you're on the path, Donna."

"George — I remember you saying the spiritual path is a lonely one because you take it by yourself."

"Yup. I said that alright and I'm not complaining, because it's the path to truth and understanding your inner self. It gives you purpose. My life shifted when I learned my purpose was to help people. Nowadays, there's so little time and so much work. I get lonely. George sipped his black coffee and sat back. "But, it's what I want to do in this lifetime. Donna, do you know how many people are in pain? I talk to people everyday who just can't get out of their own way to get on their spiritual path. They don't understand they're limiting themselves. Why, some people wouldn't know an enlightening experience if it hit them between the eyes."

I nodded and said, "I can understand that. Say, can I ask you a serious question?"

George threw up his hands and chuckled. "Here we go again. Can I still eat? I need to have enough energy to answer all those worldly questions you have burning inside. The tough ones like why are there world wars, why are people born blind, and why do people get divorced?"

"I love our philosophical sessions, but let's save it for another time," I said. " I want to talk about my decision to testify. And believe me, George, I was really attached to my decision. When I got on the stand, I was prepared and committed to the best of my ability. I overcame my fear and insecurities and my mind never wavered once from what I had to do for the victims." I took a deep breath and let it out. "I had a solid purpose and everything I had to do seemed so clear. Yeah, I guess that's it — I saw it. I had real clear vision. George, is this a one time fluke, or can I become that person again? I'm talking about the day-to-day stuff I'll have to face. Will I always have such clear vision to make the right decision? I'm talking about things like relationships." George's eyebrow arched up like a caterpillar in motion. "Okay, George, not a good example. What about work and where I should live?"

"Donna, I just lost count of all the questions I have to answer." George swallowed the last of his fish and said, "What you did today was for the highest good."

I tossed him one of my "I don't get it" looks.

"I'll explain by telling you a little story."

I scrunched up my nose and said, "Another one of those."

"That's how we learn. Simple little stories. Anyhow, this happened years back, in Oklahoma City. The cold was so bitter, it froze your teeth. I parked, went to my appointment and forgot to lock my car. When I returned, I found a drunk had crawled into the back seat and was sound asleep. A rational mind might say, 'Call the police, get him out of your car and get him out of your life.' But, I had a feeling about this guy and my gut told me he was a good man who had just gone astray with drink. So I shook him awake and, man, he was a mess. I took him to a little coffee shop on the corner. We drank I don't know how many cups of coffee. I can put the coffee away, but it was even too much for me. Well, this man named Earl told me a sad story of how he lost a successful business, his wife kicked him out and his kids had lost their respect for him — all because of his drinking.

"I asked him if he really wanted to stop drinking. He hemmed and hawed and said he'd like to stop, but he'd tried and failed several times and didn't think he could. I'm sure you get the dismal picture, Donna. I asked him if he loved his wife and family and did he want to get back with them? Earl assured me he did, but said she wouldn't take him back as long as he was drinking. Then, I asked if he wanted to be a success in business again. Earl said he needed to support his family and he liked being a success much more than he liked being a drunk. I looked him straight in the eye and said, "If you could stop drinking, get on your feet, make some money and get your family back, are you willing to help people?" Earl didn't have the foggiest idea of what I was asking and I said, "If you can stop drinking, do you suppose other people can stop drinking? Well, he thought about it and decided that if he could do it, anyone could do it. So, I made him promise me something — no money or anything like that. If I was to help him get his life back, he had to promise to reach out and help others."

"We met everyday and Earl sobered up. I bought him some clothes and got him a job. I'm not saying it was easy. He had some tough going to stay away from drinking. It was his demon. I made it a point to be there when he needed me, and sometimes when he thought he didn't. Nope, it wasn't easy. Earl had to take a hard look at his past and where he was in the present. It was my job to show him where he could go in the future and that he had real potential. Well, in time, Earl got back with his family and eventually wound up owning a huge meat packing plant."

I almost dropped my fork and said, "George, that's the Earl I met! Remember when you ran out of your cherry pipe tobacco and I had to drive all the way from Tulsa to Oklahoma City? You said you needed it for thinking. Earl had it shipped in for you and I picked it up from him. Such a nice man. Wait a minute. Isn't — isn't he the man who took to working with young people in the Alcoholics Anonymous in Oklahoma City?"

George nodded and smiled. "He's the one. He kept his promise and has helped thousands of people."

I thought for a moment about the way Earl had conquered self-pity and hopelessness to save his and so many other lives. "How did you know when this wreck of a man climbed into the back of your car that you could take him from the depths of despair and show him the light?"

"Donna, it's always up to the individual.

> **When you get sick and tired of being sick and tired, you'll change."**

Just then a very attractive couple passed by our table holding hands and laughing. "Look at that, George. I envy those two people. They seem so in love, so happy. Is that ever going to happen to me?"

George waggled his hand at me. "You're judging by what you see on the outside. Do you really know if those people are happy? Maybe they've piled up tremendous debt to look good on the out-side. How do you know they don't fight all they time? Learn to look beyond the outside. Now let's talk more about today. The person in that courtroom was who you really are. It was no mis-take. You had self-confidence and the inner vision to make the right choices. And when you're thinking about making a major change in your life, always ask if it's for your highest good."

"George, I ask questions every night, but what does for my highest good mean?"

"It's what you did in the courtroom, Donna." Highest good is what you're asking to make the best choice for you, your life, the people around you and for the relationship you have with your maker. You look confused," he said.

"I am. I still don't understand what that means," I said.

> **"Ask if it's for your highest good: spiritually, mentally, emotionally and financially.**

You want it to serve you on all levels. Will it teach you a good learning lesson? Will you grow from the experience?"

"Give me an example," I asked.

When George's eyes squinted, I knew he was thinking. After a bit, he said, "What if you see this car you really like? You say, 'I want that car'. You write out a check and buy it. What you don't know is that the engine is going to blow up in a couple of weeks, and you're going to spend a bunch of money to have it replaced. This is what you need to do when you want something: *get real clear, see it in your mind, say it out loud, and, finally, ask if it's for your highest good.* If it is, and you work for what you want, it'll happen. Sometimes fear gets in your way and you have to understand what it is you're afraid of. It takes time and faith.

> **Trust your intuition. Keep testing and trusting it. Ask questions. Everyone on the planet has the gift of insight, but we don't take the time to look inside and get the answers.**

Ask that daily question in a positive way. And expect an answer. Keep looking for it. It might come in a dream, from a friend — in some of the darnedest ways."

"Okay, George. I'm understanding inner vision, for my highest good and why I need to ask questions. Let's say I get the answer to my question. How do I make it happen?"

"George pushed his plate away, empty, but for two shriveled up french fries. "You get that higher vibration — what you call a 'knowing.' You actually focus on three levels: your sub-conscious, your conscious and then, your higher consciousness."

I tried to make sense of what he said. Sometimes, just when I thought I understood, it slipped away. This was one of those times. "Do you mean I should focus on a certain outcome?"

He nodded. "The more focused you are, the higher the vibration, and the more positive energy you have to create an outcome. If you want money in your life, you have to do more than think about it. Donna, you're a perfect example of that."

My mouth dropped open. "I am? Me?"

"You focused your energy in Hawaii. What were you doing there?"

"You know. I went to the University."

"What were you doing for a living?"

"I had some money, but it ran out and I had to sell pots and pans. But, you know all that."

"You sold your cookware, put yourself through college and got a teaching degree. And didn't you buy a sports car and travel to Europe. And didn't your cookware money help you win the title?"

"Gee, George, to listen to you, it sounds like it was all fun."

"The point is, Donna, you put yourself on the path to success. Sure, people and events will come along to try and knock you off your path. And from time to time, we all revert back to our old negative patterns. When that happens, you have to get strong inside and get moving in the right direction again."

"I understand now, " I said. "I was focusing my energy. Why didn't I learn this earlier?" I had no sooner asked the question when the answer came. "George, I think I just answered my own question. It's all so clear. The plane crash — it wasn't a mistake."

He nodded thoughtfully. "You knew from your nightmares the plane would crash, but you wouldn't slow down long enough to listen. How many nightmares came to you before the crash?"

"A bunch." It was really making sense now. "I even threw up before I left for the airport and I was the last person to board the plane. When I dreamt about what would happen to me, I tried unsuccessfully to book several other flights and wound up on the original one. What I didn't understand is, certain things are predestined and we can't change them no matter what we do."

"You got that right," George said. "You had to be on that plane. It changed your life and your destiny. Think back to when you first realized the details about the accident had to be exposed and tell me when that was."

I thought hard and said, "The visit to the burn ward convinced me. It's hard to explain how inadequate I felt. It's as if the entire experience is embedded in my memory. It's with me this very minute. The experience was so sorrowful — so real, I actually felt their heartaches and their pain. I never want that to happen to anyone ever again. It was terrible." I fought back the tears.

"It's called compassion," George said. "Compassion gave you the courage to tell your story on the witness stand and convince those important people to do something. Sometimes, we need to experience a massive life-changing event before we do something good for mankind. In your case, it got you committed to helping those victims. You envisioned yourself in that courtroom standing up for those people. All that happened to you, beginning with Mary Margaret's call to the nurse, was no coincidence."

The pent-up tears streamed down my cheeks.

George pushed his plate away and sighed. "It's okay to cry, Donna," he said softly and handed me his handkerchief. "You've been through a lot. I guess you're not going to finish that plate of food," he said. I shook my head. He reached for his pipe and rose from his chair. "I need a smoke."

Coming out of the restaurant, I decided I had a trunk-load of lessons for one day. George was heading for the ice-cream booth like he was on a mission.

"What flavor are you going to have, Donna?"

"I don't know. Maybe not any. I don't feel like it."

George stopped in his tracks. "I don't think I've ever heard you turn down ice-cream before. Humph. Well, I'm going to have vanilla — maybe strawberry."

I wiped my tears, blew my nose. "Boring, George. Maybe, I'll just have a little chocolate chip fudge. Are you having one scoop or two?"

George put a match to his pipe and began puffing. He blew out sweet smelling smoke and said, "I'm getting a Santa belly. One is enough for me."

I said, "You're the kindest man I know. You'd make a great Santa Claus. I'm going to have two scoops. I want mocha coffee on top of the chocolate chip fudge — with chocolate sprinkles. Hey, why the weird look?"

George grinned and said, "Not me. I wouldn't look weird."

I turned toward the sea and inhaled the cool salty air. "Look out there, George. The white sand, the sparkling blue water, all those people having fun. Isn't life beautiful?"

George paused to study the panoramic view of the splendid Pacific, the sea-gulls dipping into the water against a backdrop of sun-bathed sky. "Yes, Donna," he said, a faraway look in his eyes, "life is very beautiful."

JOURNAL
For My Highest Good

So much has happened. *Now that I have been through major life-changing events, how do I start healing, put my life together and move forward?* If I am to move ahead, I'll need to clarify what I learned today and make sure I understand. George and I talked about the pain and how my visit to the burn ward gave me the compassion I needed to take the witness stand. I did it for my fellow passenger's highest good, but I also did it for me. I discovered a part of me I didn't know I had.

When I want something, I must first ask my inner self the question and then ask if it's for my highest good. Sometimes I can just think about the question and other times, I can say it out loud. I'm learning to trust my higher consciousness and the answers I receive. I know the answer lies within me. If I feel anxious and uneasy, whatever caused that feeling is not for my highest good. There are times when I ask a question and a calmness settles over me. I sense the worries lift and my spirit grow confident. And there are those inexplicable times when I ramble off questions, one after another, and the answers come in a blast of certainty.

I'm aware that no great life ascent was ever made without stumbles and falls, and plenty of them. The plane crash was the most powerful lesson on love I have ever learned. When I was subpoenaed, I didn't think it was in my best interest to be grilled and cross examined by all the people from the airline industry. By experiencing the pain the victims felt, I learned compassion and gained the strength to testify. My questions to the Universe are: *How do I keep the momentum of moving forward on my path? Who will I become?*

Thank you Universe. I have been through massive change and I claim my purpose.

I will do what is for my highest good spiritually, mentally, emotionally and financially.

SECTION II

THE HEALING

The Power
Of Mentors

I had always dreamed of helicopter skiing in the Canadian Caraboos. Long before the plane crash, I had booked the ski trip for myself and a group of friends. I visualized basking in crystal clear days, surrounded by acres of untouched snow and skiing down the mountain, white powder billowing behind me.

Only six weeks after the crash and I couldn't believe I was here at last. The Caraboos were even more beautiful than I imagined. I stood on the summit, enveloped by a sea of silence and a landscape unchanged by evolution. The snow glistened like diamonds and a blazing sun glazed the mountain peaks vanilla white. I couldn't help thinking that the awe-inspiring view and my being here was great, but the timing was all wrong. My back and legs were still healing and I worried they weren't strong enough to handle rugged mountain skiing.

Cliff was part of our ski group and a man I had once dated. Though no longer a couple, I thought we were friends. The consummate television producer, his idea of success was owning an expensive car, having an exemplary wardrobe, dining at the finest restaurants and draping a glamorous woman on his arm. He valued his material "stuff." I stood gazing at the natural wonders that no amount of money could buy and couldn't help but question his reason for being here. I knew there was a lesson to be learned. I just didn't know if it was for him, or for me.

The last time I saw Cliff was just before the plane crash. We had spent the day at Mammoth Ski Resort and I was starving after a morning of skiing. When we sat down to eat, I commented I could eat one of everything on the menu, but would settle for a burger with the works and french fries.

Cliff let his eyes wander to my thighs. "You aren't going to eat all that are you? I've noticed you've put on a few pounds," he said disdainfully.

His reference to my figure left me feeling fat and unattractive. So much so, I ordered a small salad and water. Cliff ordered the works. I was seething when the waiter placed a huge burger, fries and a chocolate milkshake in front of him. During lunch, I saw his eyes spark with interest. The subject of his admiration was a brunette wearing skin-tight designer togs. In his own insensitive way, Cliff was rejecting me. Throughout our relationship, his producing career and everything connected with it came first. And I was nothing but a replaceable starlet who had decided to write off her dead-end relationship with him.

But I wasn't about to cancel a spectacular ski-trip because of a man whose values conflicted with mine. Instead, I was ecstatic because I was in the middle of nowhere, between Vancouver and Calgary, and about to experience the best skiing in the world.

A tall, slim man in his late thirties, wearing a bright red ski suit introduced himself as Raimund, our guide. His eyes were deep blue, the color of clear mountain lakes and his tanned face was framed by blond hair. He pointed to the helicopter and directed us on board.

Riding in a helicopter for the first time, I felt light-headed and nauseated. Not from fear but more from a ripple of expectancy over what could happen. I eventually mustered up the courage to look out the window. The scenery was breathtaking. No civilization, just pristine snow covered peaks, one after another. An unspoiled paradise cloaked in peaceful solitude. I felt thankful just to be alive.

The only negative was Cliff, acting as if we were still an item and he, Mr. Wonderful. I almost laughed when I saw him express a smile of approval as he looked me up and down. Little did he know that my weight loss was the result of post-crash stress.

The helicopter put us off at the top of the world, on a flat mountain that descended straight down on three sides.

"Pair up!" Raimund ordered in his clipped European accent.

Cliff yelled, "Donna, we're partners."

I nodded vaguely. He was a good skier. Raimund handed out little yellow beepers and explained in a clipped accent how to use them in case we were buried in an avalanche. "Never ski alone and never ski before your guide. Wait always until I tell you to come."

An accomplished skier, Raimund moved like quicksilver down the mountain. Part way to the bottom, he stopped, raised his ski pole high in the air and swung it around. Our signal to follow. Dazzling powder flew in all directions as my companions barreled down the mountain with Cliff in the lead, yelling at the top of his lungs. He knew I was not over my injuries, yet he had not bothered to wait for me. It was his way of sending me a message that I couldn't ski as well as him and would hold him back. The run was his, and without me. He'd flattened my confidence like a burst balloon. Alone, and a little frightened without any support, I pushed off. The snow was soft as satin and beautiful like no other I had ever experienced, but I struggled with every turn. When I reached the group where Cliff was waiting, I wiped out and tumbled down at Raimund's feet. The group laughed at my clumsiness. I got to my feet and brushed myself off. I felt the heat of embarrassment flood my cheeks and forced down the urge to ski away from everyone.

"It is tricky. Don't worry. You do fine," Raimund reassured me.

He turned and again skied ahead. When he signaled, I hung to the back of the group and skied fairly well, considering my bad ankle. All I ever glimpsed of Cliff was the back of his head. Each downhill run required a helicopter ride back up the mountain. By the third helicopter ride, I had gained more confidence in the helicopter and in myself.

Our group met for a brown bag lunch at a wonderful clearing atop a favorite mountain. The sun had warmed the snow to frosty perfection, the view was magnificent and it was the moment we were all waiting for. A full 5300-foot run Raimund had pegged the "Legburner."

Raimund looked at me and said, "Donna, you ski with me."

I was shocked. I sensed he considered me a rather substandard skier and I felt threatened by how the others had reacted earlier when I fell. "No," I protested, "I really can't do this."

"Yes, you can," he said, gazing at me with his penetrating blue eyes. I do one half of a figure eight and you follow my tracks to make the other half."

My mind kept protesting. *I can't do it — I just can't do it.* Raimund and I were separated from the rest of the group while they split up to prepare. I shook my head and said, "I'm sorry, Raimund, but I'm in no shape to follow you down the mountain. Let me stay toward the rear and then if I fall, no one will see me and make fun of me."

"I've been watching and you can do it, but only if you want. Live in the moment, Donna. Why be afraid of what anyone thinks," Raimund said. "You ski well. Relax, stay within your center and be one with the mountain. Go for it while you have chance — live."

Cliff walked over just then and said, "Donna is skiing with me, Raimund."

Raimund shook his head. "No. You have never stayed with her once today. She will ski with me and I can know she is okay. You go last down the mountain."

"You'll make a fool of yourself, Donna," Cliff murmured, low enough for just me to hear.

Cliff didn't know it, but he had done me a favor. That was the moment I made up my mind not to run from the challenge and to follow Raimund down the mountain. All my life I'd run from what I wanted and had settled for second best. I'd been ruled by fear that I wasn't good enough, or that I would fail, so what was the use trying? This single moment offered me a chance to break that pattern. Staying in the background wouldn't build my confidence. I had to believe in myself — that I was a winner, no matter what.

Raimund adjusted his goggles and gave me a long, meaningful look. I watched him shove off and begin his effortless turns, one after another across the new-fallen snow. It was obvious he was one with the mountain and the outdoors his natural domain.

I shoved off and began my turns, carving through Raimund's figure eights. The heat in my thighs intensified with each turn, and pain shot through my ankle, but the reward of accomplishment was worth the pain. I followed his tracks like I was dancing in a snow ballet. The tools were all there. I believed in myself — that I could do it and I did. Breathless and grinning, I slid to a stop within an inch of Raimund's ski tips. "I did it, Raimund," I shouted. I did it!" At that moment, I felt happier than I had in a long time. The searing pain in my thighs didn't matter because, like the mountain, the message emerged crystal clear. " I just had to go for it."

"He gave me a hug and said, "Life is not so bad, eh Donna? It is pretty terrific." The sun was setting and the moon rising when we made our last run down the mountain. It was a great day — the best skiing in my life.

Alerted by the quick moving clouds we made it back to the lodge just as the blizzard started. Our snowbound group milled around playing pool, or writing post cards. I soaked my aching muscles in the hot tub. I wanted to avoid Cliff.

Dinner was a delicious feast of roast beef, heaps of mashed potatoes, gravy and home-made pie. After dinner, Raimund called me over to his table where he was making helicopter schedules for the next day. As I passed, Cliff gave me a grumpy look that implied I had something scandalous going on with our guide.

Raimund motioned for me to sit down and said, "Not so goot with him, no?"

I shook my head and sighed. "Not for a long time. Seems I always pick men who are emotionally unavailable."

"Donna, why you sell yourself short?"

His words offended me, at first. Then, I realized Raimund was only demonstrating concern. I shrugged and said, "I can't re-member a time when I didn't feel this way. I've spent my entire life trying to look the best and be the best. It's the only time I really feel liked — or loved. I never thought anyone could really care about the person who was plain old me." I sighed heavily. "The plane crash compelled me to change. I know I can't con-tinue being someone I'm not. I need to be me and yet, Raimund, I don't quite know how to do that."

Raimund smiled and squeezed my hand. "Relax. The answers come. By the way, you ski with Mike tomorrow."

"What about you?" I asked, feeling a little wounded.

"I ski with slow group." He smiled, nodded. "You do fine where you are."

The next day was again a glorious and memorable ski time. However, my back injury was aggravated and I tired before the rest of the group. Cliff made it a point to call me a quitter when I decided to return to the lodge with the helicopter refueling team.

I went right to my room and took a long nap. Later that afternoon, one of the group woke me and asked if I wanted to go to the guide's house for a sauna. It sounded wonderful. The house was actually a small chalet overlooking a lake and just a short drive from our cabin area.

I lasted only twenty minutes in the 145 degree sauna. When I saw no sign of Raimund, I asked where he was and another guide gave me directions to his room. I walked up the steps and down the hall to the second door on the left. I knocked softly and a sleepy voice answered, "Ya?"

"Raimund, it's Donna."

The door opened and there he stood, barefoot, wearing only his blue jeans. I lowered my eyes, feeling embarrassed.

"Come in," he said and opened the door wider. "What a surprise."

His big smile made me feel a little more at ease. I entered his room and said, "I just finished baking in the sauna and decided to come up and say, hi."

"Your cheeks are rosy."

He wouldn't know it was a flush of sudden shyness.

Raimund patted the bed, his tone serious. "Come sit. We talk." I sat down on the edge of the bed and waited for him to say something. "I like you, Donna," he continued, "and I think of you — too often. You see, I am married."

I reflected on what he'd said and on the barren third finger of his left hand. How could I know he was married? But, perhaps in other countries, a man's wedding ring wasn't such a big deal. I felt foolish and said, "Oh Raimund, I didn't know."

He gazed deep into my eyes and said, "I could be with you. My wife never know. But, is not honest. I would know. I promise her if she stay in Austria and work and I come to Canada and work, we trust each other. We have much deep love. If I do wrong, I would be dishonest with her and myself. I am not the man for you, Donna. He will come — someday."

Raimund's blue eyes revealed a warm glow when he spoke of his wife and I realized the tremendous difference between Cliff and Raimund. Cliff communicated in a way that was indifferent and often hurtful. When Raimund spoke, he gave me insight and a breath of hope. I smiled and said, "It's okay. I understand what you mean. But, I'd sure like to know when 'he' will happen."

"When time is right, Donna," he said sincerely. "Nature is best healer. You are doing right. When you heal inside and center yourself, your vibration attracts."

I wanted to understand, to know more. "Raimund, what do you mean by vibration?"

He frowned, rubbed his palms together like he was amassing the right words.

> "When you are on higher consciousness, you attract a man who is on higher consciousness. When that happens, you know. But first, be kind to yourself, respect yourself and be with nature. Know you have great worth."

I glanced at Raimund and sighed. "When you say nature, do you mean God?"

"I mean little of both, Donna. They are one." He stood, held out his hand and smiled. "Now, I take you back to your cabin."

During the ride back to the group quarters, Raimund asked questions about the plane crash I had only alluded to in earlier conversations. When we reached the cabin, he gave me a big hug and said, "Do not worry, Donna. You are learning magic of life." He leaned over and kissed my cheek.

I paused at the door of the cabin when I saw the curtain flutter at the window. A light blinked on and Cliff threw open the door.

His face flamed beet red beneath his recent tan. "You were with him! We have to talk! Now! I'm tired of you making me look like an idiot."

I tossed him a disgusted look.

"You have to be with the best looking guide, the best skier. You won't be with me, Miss La De Da, but you spent the afternoon making love with *him*. Didn't you? Answer me," Cliff insisted.

His words were raw and angry. I stared at him and calmly said, "I won't waste my breath explaining, Cliff, because you are incapable of understanding."

A look of surprise crossed his face and he softened his demeanor. "I care about you, Donna. I thought this trip would get us back together."

His whiny tone seemed artificial, almost pathetic. "Too late, Cliff. You don't care about me. All that matters to you is to be first. And when you look at me, all you see is whether I match your idea of the perfect woman." I didn't want to hold back any longer. I wanted him to know exactly how I felt about him. "Actually, it doesn't matter what you think anymore. If I got sick or needed you in a crisis, would you be there for me?" Cliff's blank stare was my answer. I said, "Just as I thought. Love is not emotional to you, it's an obligation. Cliff, you and I are history." I suddenly felt I had to get away from him. Actually, he took care of that for me.

"Have it your way," he shot back. "I'm going to dinner — without you." He walked out and slammed the door so hard the pictures on the wall shook.

The morning of our final day was glorious. The fresh lie of snow was fluffy and exquisite. My skis swept down the mountain on wings and I was charged with immense energy. When it came time to leave our enchanted wilderness, I was surprised to see Raimund packed up and ready to join us on the bus.

"I am flying from Vancouver tonight," he said, "returning to Austria."

When the bus arrived, Cliff broke from the group to board behind me. He nudged me to the back of the bus and took the seat next to me. I didn't want to be around him. But, when I stood up to move, he blocked my way with his arm.

"You're making a fool of me. You're not sitting with *him*," Cliff blurted out.

I was furious and didn't care who heard me. I said loud enough for the entire bus to hear, "Let me out, Cliff — now." I meant business and he knew it. He dropped his arm down and I slid past.

I hurried to the front of the bus and sat down beside Raimund.

He smiled briefly and said, "He is, as you say, history?"

I chuckled. "You bet." I felt self-conscious after our last discussion, but it was most likely the last time I would see Raimund and I had to say what was in my heart. "This will most likely be the last time we talk, Raimund, and I want to ask you something that's been on my mind for some time."

He turned to me with an intense expression. "Ask."

"Why is it when I first met you, I instantly felt like I knew you. It's hard to explain how drawn to you I felt. It seemed so natural and, sure enough, you became a good friend and advisor."

He nodded, smiled. "Maybe in past lifetime we know each other."

"What?"

"Perhaps I was your teacher, your guide. People get special insight. It's gift."

After we had arrived back in town and I was leaving the bus, Raimund turned to me with a knowing look behind his brilliant blue eyes and said, "In another lifetime, Donna, we meet again."

✈ ✈ ✈

Almost six months had passed since the crash. My life and I had changed in many ways, but I was still a budding actress who believed thin and beautiful would insure success. My body was screaming for help. After years of bulimic behavior and taking diet pills, I had to get healthy. The problem — I didn't have the foggiest idea how to establish nutritious eating patterns, or even what a *basic* exercise program meant. I would exercise like crazy all week and the next week, I'd stuff myself with junk food and drag around afterwards. My energy barometer was bouncing up and down and I knew that it was crucial to get myself in balance quickly.

My seeds of bulimia were sown early in life by my mother, who regularly reminded me when I had gained a few pounds, and later, by finicky men in Hollywood who would only date size six women. I became obsessive about my weight. I ate any food I wanted and then, threw up everything I had eaten. I knew it was only a matter of time before my eating disorder became life threatening.

In the past, I'd beat myself up for solutions I didn't have. The plane crash forced me tolook at myself, who I really was, but I hadn't learned the skills to eliminate my negative patterns. I was in the 'seek and heal' time of life. When you can't help yourself, you turn to the people who can help you.

So, I signed myself up for a month long endurance program at the Ashram Health Resort, nestled in the mountains of Calabasas, California. I was told not to bring my own car and that the Ashram's driver would pick me up at my apartment and drive me to the resort. When he turned down a long winding dirt road, I gazed around at my surroundings and it dawned on me that it was a very long walk to the nearest fast food. Then, I reminded myself again of the purpose behind my enrolling — to learn how to eat healthy and get physically strong again.

I was dropped off in front of a large rustic house and told to go inside. I entered the front door that led into an spacious main room. Above the fireplace a carved wooden sign occupied most of the wall and read:

> Be still and know I am God.
> Be still and know I am.
> Be still and know I.
> Be still and know.
> Be still.
> Be.

At that moment, I knew my sojourn would be more than a physical experience. Just as I'd thought the plane crash was entirely a struggle to survive, it had also given me spiritual enlightenment. The Ashram, I was to learn, was another challenging path to wisdom and love.

The main house had five bedrooms, kitchen, dining room and a large living room. There were eight women in all enrolled. Two people were bunked in each of the plain but practical bedrooms.

I was given an orange sweat suit and told I would receive a clean one each morning. I grinned at the irony of the situation. I had always been on the vain side about wearing certain colors. This particular orange color, with my red hair, made me look like a fruit compote. Still, I was impatient to get on with the program.

A tall, blond, Swedish woman introduced herself as Catharina, the director of the Ashram. Beautiful and energetic, her face glowed with good health and laughter enlivened her brown eyes.

"Ja. Ja, ladies," she said after appraising our little group, "we are here for fun. Can you believe it?"

A woman, who was a previous recruit, whispered that Catharina was dubbed the 'laughing saint.' And when Catharina disclosed her age, it was hard to believe this together woman was only a year older than I.

Our day began with a 6:00 a.m. wake-up. Sunlight streamed down on the mountains outside my window as I struggled into my orange sweat suit. I plodded over to the meditation dome mumbling to myself and asking what I was doing at this forsaken place.

I did not anticipate the pleasant experience that awaited me. Inside the dome, hundreds of crystals swung from the ceiling, bathing us in a spectrum of light. The high-pitched chant of flute music gave me a sense of tranquil reassurance. I sat on a pillow, closed my eyes and envisioned myself in a sanctuary where real peace meant letting go of tension and enjoying the place and the moment. That day was the first of many soul-searching encounters in the dome of light.

I was famished and ready for the lumberman's special by the time I headed back to the house for breakfast. A large glass of orange juice sat at each of our places. I gulped mine straight down and glanced expectantly toward the kitchen.

"Ja. Ja. We go now." Catharina burst into the room laughing. "Straight up the mountain. Can you believe it?"

Now I understood why Catharina kept cowbells on the refrigerator door. She didn't want her starving inmates to raid it.

The heat fumed intense by eight o'clock in the morning. We trotted behind Catharina, up a vertical, dusty fire path lined with dense bushes. As I pushed and wheezed up the mountain, it became apparent I was terribly out of shape. I tugged at the collar of my sweat shirt and admonished myself for paying money to be treated like I was in a detention facility. As I drifted into a fuzzy haze, I began to understand the lesson from this experience. It had to do with persistence and putting one blistered foot before the other — all the way to the top of the mountain.

Eight miles later, we staggered into the main house and collapsed on the couches. My eyes were sandy, my bones ached and my plane crash injuries were throbbing. I glanced around at the other women and wondered if sweat had formed dust trails down my cheeks, and if my hair was glued to my scalp. I leaned my head back and fantasized taking a cool shower. I was drinking my second glass of water when I heard the sound of Catharina's laughter. I sat straight up.

"Ja. Ja. Time for weight lifting, ladies," Catharina said with such eagerness, I could have strangled her, but I was too exhausted to even lift my hands. "This is Maxie, your trainer." I looked up to see a short, muscular man enter the room. Like Catharina, he also radiated health and energy.

Within minutes, we were lifting 30-pound weights. Maxie stopped at my work-out station and grinned. I detected the strong scent of garlic when he said with a slight accent, "Everyday I vill increase your veights. You vill be strong and trim. Veights are the best to tone the body."

I grunted a response. I had considered myself to be about ten pounds overweight, but in fair shape. Here it was only ten o'clock in the morning, and I was on the verge of collapse. My legs felt like cooked noodles and my arms trembled from exertion. I blinked back tears and wished my mustang would show up to rescue me.

"Ja. Ja. Swimming pool. Ten minutes! Can you believe it?"

I sighed with relief. A relaxing dip in cool water. Would any-one notice if I crawled to the pool and jumped in with my sweats on? I put on my swim suit and discovered it was not to be a sunbathing session. We were there to play water volleyball.

The water temperature was just at the melting point of ice-cubes. Wild and uncoordinated, our flailing efforts kept us from dying of hypothermia. Catharina must have thought we had re-cuperated because she insisted we play two games.

Throughout Catharina's regime of health and fitness exer-cises, I found myself trying to analyze her. Her zest for life was obviously sincere and her radiant beauty was not bought at a cos-metic counter. Perhaps if I studied her closely, I could learn her secret to happiness.

After water volleyball, we donned our shapeless white robes and convened for lunch. Six cantaloupe halves garnished with a dollop of plain yogurt and all the water we could drink. I gobbled up every morsel.

"Ja. Ja."

What now? I wondered. Calisthenics in the noonday sun?

"Massage and two-hour rest period. Sleep well, ladies."

A therapeutic massage put fresh life into my aching muscles. I dragged myself to bed and was asleep within minutes.

When we woke, we were told to go outside, pick up eight pebbles and begin our jog around the track. At the end of each lap, our instructions were to drop a pebble into a can located beneath a large willow tree. After just four laps, I considered depositing two pebbles at a time. But, the affection and respect for the woman who was fast becoming my inspiration would not allow me to cheat. I huffed an exasperated sigh and dropped a single pebble into the can.

"Ja, you are doing great, Donna," Catharina called out, trot-ting past me. "Keep it up." She laughed. "Just one more mile."

My exhaustion grew by the minute, but the show went on. Next on the agenda was a three-mile hike.

"Smile," Catharina joked. " No hills, all flat — an easy hike. Go at your own pace and it will be fun. Can you believe it?"

Now why couldn't I believe a three-mile hike would be fun?

We returned from the hike dusty, sweaty, and beyond collapse.

"Ja. Ladies. Here we go! Up on the roof for aerobics."

I thought it was some weird joke until I heard the sound of disco music wafting down from the roof. Bleary eyed and dog tired, I dragged myself up the steps. Too beat to even speak, I shuffled through the routines like a rag doll, not caring what I looked like, or whether I was in sync with the music. I noticed two of the women slouched down on a sit-down strike. I did even better. When the music stopped, I sprawled spread eagle down on the mat.

The next I knew, Catharina was shaking me awake.

"Wake up sleepyhead. I have a treat in store for you."

Ah, food, I thought.

"It is relaxation and yoga in the meditation dome."

"I can't move," I answered.

"Ja. You can." Catharina laughed, reached for my hands and pulled me to my feet.

"Clear your mind of negative thoughts. Visualize yourself at your end result: healthy, active and in good shape," she said steering me up the path to the dome.

> "When change happens from the inside, the outside changes."

In spite of myself, I had to admit Catharina was right. After a day at the Ashram's exhausting boot camp, yoga in the meditation dome had reduced my fatigue and I could focus again.

Dinner that night was a huge salad. The vegetables were the most sumptuous I had ever tastedand I savored each crunchy bite. It didn't bother me in the least when we went to bed before dark.

To me, salvation was making it through the day. And each day was much the same as the last. Only the fruit and vegetables we were served varied. Even now I remember how our conversations focused on food. About the fourth day, I noticed our attitudes had changed. We no longer complained and laughed off our aches and pains. We marched up the side of the mountain with purpose and energy. We even ate our food slower, enjoying it more. We didn't bother with make-up, or fuss with our hair, but we were childishly happy.

At weigh-in I learned I had shed only three pounds after such a grueling week. Women who were heavier had lost up to ten pounds. My hopes sank and I discussed my feelings with Catharina.

"Don't worry, Donna," she assured me waving away my displeasure. You are doing fabulous! Your metabolism burns slow. Ja, you will lose at a slower pace. You need plenty of exercise and lots of water to increase your metabolic rate. Most important is to get your body healthy. Soon, your skin will radiate good health, your hair will shine and your eyes will be so clear. It takes time to rid your body of the junk food and to replace the vitamins lost from the bulimia. You must work to find your own path to health. Can you believe it?"

One afternoon after we'd sat down for lunch in our t-shirts and sweat pants, a new guest was introduced as a reporter from Vogue magazine. We stared at her in awe. She wore cosmetics, was glamorous and every lacquered hair stayed perfectly in place. I gulped down my juice, wolfed down my tuna stuffed papaya and even ate the papaya skin while Miss Vogue sat across from me, watching, appalled.

Two days later, I didn't blink an eye when I saw her disheveled and eating her papaya skin. That was the beauty of the Ashram. It diminished the judgement side in all of us.

By the end of the third week, the physical change in myself I longed for had happened. I was firm and toned, my skin wore a healthy glow and the luster was restored to my hair. Though still tired at the end of the day, I leapt out of bed each morning, eager to challenge myself, to test my strength and be with nature.

In the fourth week, I was thrilled when my friend, Brooke, showed up at Fort Ashram and we became room mates. She was close to my age, vivacious, and a flight attendant. Since we each had an outrageous sweet tooth, I wondered how she would take to the Ashram's holistic diet..

One hot day on the fire trail, I glanced behind me and saw Brooke trudging up the trail in her orange sweat suit looking like a wilted marigold. I remembered vividly my first days at the Ashram, but as I grew strong toughened and toned, each day got easier — as it would for Brooke. I quickened my pace until I was beside Catharina. I gave her a high sign. Jogging beside Catharina, my heart pounded, but my chest no longer burned; my gait had turned light-footed and steady. I glanced at her face, aglow with serenity and it seemed the right time to ask what had been on my mind since I arrived.

I said, "Catharina, who or what makes you so happy?"

She stopped jogging, sat down on a nearby rock and gestured for me to sit next to her. We each took a moment to catch our breath and have a cool drink of water before she said, "Donna, don't you know yet? No one thing or person can make you happy. Only you can bring happiness to yourself."

I glanced over at her and sighed in exasperation "I've heard that one before, but what does it mean? How do I make *me* happy? I can't give myself acting jobs."

Catharina bowed her head and smiled a yes. "First, learn who you are. Many people who come to the Ashram believe they are here only for the physical gains — to get in shape. But to accept and heal the body, one needs awareness of spirit — the power of body and spirit working on all levels together. The closer they are, the better." She waggled her finger at me. "But, you cannot let the outer control the inner. Ja?"

"And how do I do that?" I asked.

Catharina nodded. "For almost a month, Donna, I have listened to you say, 'I am so in need of feeling loved by a man,' and then, you ask why you cannot find a man to love you. Do you want to know why?"

I hung my head, afraid to hear what this woman who had earned my greatest admiration would say.

She put her hand beneath my chin and looked me in the eye. "Because you don't love yourself. Once you love yourself and send that energy out, the right man will accept you for who you are, despite any shortcomings. Don't ever be afraid to show the real you. You can't pretend to be someone else to make men like you."

Catharina rose and started back up the trail, saying over her shoulder.

"Truth lies behind all things. Find it, but do not judge yourself. Be."

As I followed Catharina up the mountain, her long strides one to each of my two, I pondered over what she had said. George had said the same thing:

"Learn to love and accept yourself."

I understood the philosophy. I was even putting it into practice by doing good for other people and taking small steps to love myself. Yet, I still doubted if I was worthy enough for someone else to love me. I had not totally claimed the philosophy behind *love and accept yourself*, but I questioned my beliefs.

That night, a full moon floated in the sky above the Ashram. My introspective mood lingered and I couldn't sleep. I kept recalling hurtful memories from long ago. There were two dark sides to my family, one side personified alcohol and the other violence — a breeding ground for abandonment.

My first time in a hospital was at age six. My father traveled and was frequently away from home. He often neglected to leave my mother money and we ate a lot of noodles. My brother contracted scarlet fever, and I was hospitalized with malnutrition. During my recovery, my mother filed for divorce. From the day of the divorce, my parents never spoke to one another. The experience left me feeling guilty because I blamed myself.

At age sixteen I was diagnosed as having a heart valve disorder. My father believed he was doing the right thing by insisting I have heart surgery. He drove me to a Philadelphia hospital and instructed my mother to stay away. During the surgery, I almost died from a blood clot. When I woke up in recovery, neither one of my parents was there. I felt abandoned, confused and alone in a strange place. I assumed no one loved or wanted me and I questioned why I was even on the earth. Uncovering that answer is what kept me going in the tough days ahead. Because I'd received no support from those close to me, I had to learn the rules of survival on my own.

Thinking back to those troubled days always left my insides churning. I finally gave up on trying to sleep and climbed out of bed. I moved quietly down the stairs and headed for the main room. I had just sat down on the sofa to contemplate the full meaning of the sign above the fireplace when I heard soft footsteps in the kitchen. The jangle of cow bells meant only one thing — the refrigerator door. I jumped up and peeked around the doorway in time to see Catharina running down the stairs. Whoever was raiding the refrigerator was asking for a tongue lashing.

"Brookie! Brookie! What are you doing, Brookie? I want to know. Are you eating something?" Catharina said in a commanding voice.

When I heard Brooke's muffled response, I shook my head and couldn't help but smile. Her sweet tooth had gotten the best of her.

The neon ceiling light came on in the kitchen and Catharina zeroed in. "What do you have in your mouth, Brookie? Are you eating the staff's leftover birthday cake?"

"Umph-uh." Brooke stood in the doorway, cheeks bulging like a chipmunk, shaking her head vigorously. Then, she made a dash for the bathroom and slammed the door shut behind her. Soon after that, I heard the toilet flush.

Catharina stood outside the bathroom door with her arms crossed. "Brookie," she called, "the cake is down the toilet?"

After a few seconds of Brooke's not answering, Catharina turned and walked into the main room where I was sitting and eyed me suspiciously, "Donna, were you eating cake too?" Something in my eyes must have prompted her to say, "No — I think you were after something else. What are you doing here sitting by yourself?"

"Can't sleep," I said. "Since our conversation today, I keep thinking about my mother, father and my brother."

"What about them?" Catharina said softly.

"They influenced so many of my decisions. I love my family, Catharina. I believe they love me, each in their own way. But, it always bothered me that congratulations, praise, or even a compliment was such a rarity in our household. I could only assume I wasn't worthy of any of those things and I grew up with no self-esteem. In the days before the plane crash, I had zero self-worth and actually had a death wish. When I think back, I took the path of least resistance and wound up on the road to self-destruction" I shook my head slowly and said, "I don't want to go there ever again."

Catharina placed her hand on my arm and said, "You don't have to.

> **Childhood misery often blocks the joy from adulthood."**

"What you have learned from your past and what you believe today can alter your future, Donna. But, the past is not where you should waste your precious time on this earth."

"I can't help it," I protested. "I know I have to heal with the past if I plan on having a decent future. It still hurts to think about how living with my family left me so vulnerable. After the divorce, my parents were constantly in and out of court fighting over custody of my brother and me. I tried to get along with both my parents, but they acted like they hated each other.

"Then, when I was only five months away from turning eighteen and visiting my father on weekends, a major milestone took place that caused a break in our relationship. I was expected at his house and from there to attend ski race training. My heart operation had caused an unanticipated glitch in my Olympic training and I was working hard on a comeback. The car broke down three times on the way to my father's house and I was late. When I walked in the door, he never asked why I was late, but proceeded to hit me again and again. When he finally stopped his raging, I ran to my bedroom and burrowed in the corner of the closet. I felt sick over what had just happened. The bruises were throbbing and I don't know how long I sat there crying. I agonized over whether to see my father on weekends so I could continue training for the Olympics, or stay away and become my own person. I thought the Olympics was the most important thing in my life, but after what had just happened, not being controlled by someone else was even more important.

"I returned to the room where my father was sitting. "'I'm leaving this house,' I announced. Then, I walked out the door. He never said a word. I had withstood my last beating and had mustered up the courage to break away. The willful, tenacious side of me was intact and had served me well. The unworthy side of me was still screaming for love and acceptance."

"I understand," Catharina said. "What happened after that?"

"After that, I lived at my mother's full time. In many ways she meant well and her heart was in the right place. She always prepared my favorite meals, accepted my friends into our home, paid for my dance lessons and she loved to go clothes shopping with me. Though, she always seemed overcritical of me. Once, while trying on clothes at our favorite shop, I pirouetted out of the dressing room wearing a lovely brown pants outfit.

"'Oh yes, Donna, you should wear that,' mother said. 'It's dark and doesn't make you look fat.'

"I couldn't believe my ears — couldn't believe how years of drinking had made her so judgmental. In her eyes, I would never be successful, so why would I want to become an actress. I said, 'Mother, this is a size ten. I diet, take diet pills and even throw up to be thin. Can't you say I look good?'

"Astonished, my mother said, 'You mean you throw up your food?'

"'Yes.' I answered and hung my head.

"'Well, diet pills and throwing up didn't do any good,' she said, 'you're still fat.'

"I wanted reassurance from her, but instead, her harsh words had devastated me. As usual, I locked my feelings up inside. I actually talked myself into believing my mother was right and that I should diet down to a size smaller. I wanted to get along with my family and had convinced myself only I was responsible for making that happen.

"For two years following high school graduation, I worked my way through the University of Montana by teaching skiing. I still thought about my father a lot. Since the day I walked away from his house, our conversations were infrequent and filled with tension. One day he called to say if I would spend time with him that summer, he would help with my college expenses. He had a history of broken promises, and yet, I really wanted to believe him. I explained how excited I was about transferring to the University of Hawaii. He'd always promised to help me with college, but when the time came, he backed down, saying he was financially strapped. I didn't like having to shuffle back and forth between my mother and father again, but I genuinely loved my parents and wanted our relationships to work. So I pushed aside our past problems and decided to spend time with my father that summer."

"Shortly before I was to leave for Hawaii, my father called to say he'd be out of town for a while, but my tuition check was in the mail. My mother had already warned me not to count on his help. She said he couldn't be trusted. When the envelope arrived from my father, I turned to my mother and said, 'See, he is paying for school.' I tore open the envelope and stared at the check in disbelief. I fought back waves of anger and denial and tried to believe the check wasn't made out to the University of Montana. It was a nothing but a useless piece of paper for my tuition in Hawaii and my father knew that. Tears of disappointment welled up and rolled down my cheeks. I said aloud, 'He will never betray me again.' I wrote on the front of it, 'I am going to Hawaii' and mailed it back to him. I was fed up with my parents venting their anger for each other on me. My father never reissued the check and I sold pots and pans to get my education."

All this time Catharina sat quietly listening to me pour my heart out. I turned to her and said, "I decided if people didn't love me, I would make myself worthy of love." I was silent for a moment and then I asked, "Catharina, how do you stop feeling you were never loved? How do you believe you're worthy enough to be loved by anyone? I felt it in the plane crash, but I haven't felt it since."

Catharina thought for a moment and said to me:

> "Your virtue lies in having the faith and courage to overcome the difficulties in life. Love yourself and know you are worthy, or you wouldn't be here. Begin your healing from within. Create your own love, your own life, surround yourself with people who love and accept you. Be with God."

I gazed intently at this woman, a living example of who I wanted to become. "I feel more saddened than anything else. I just don't want to transmit any of my parent's patterns to my children."

"That's good. Because your parents didn't express their love for you in the way you wanted doesn't mean you can't demonstrate genuine love to a child someday." A warm smile spread over Catharina's face and she said, "Release. You have already begun. It's why you're here at the Ashram. You are replacing an unhealthy lifestyle with healthy behavior. You are healing."

I nodded. "Your words are so comforting, Catharina. "There's so much to heal. I believed I could love myself and feel better if I was thin and that kind of dangerous thinking caused my bulimia and rotten eating habits. I thought men would like me better and I was only fooling myself. It was all make believe — just like Hollywood. I don't understand how I made so many mistakes with men. I always tried to look good, have a sense of humor. You know, the perfect companion. I figured they'd have to love me, but they never did."

Catharina shrugged. "You chose unworthy men because you felt unworthy. Forgive your mistakes and don't be so hard on yourself. When you love and accept yourself, a man will love and accept you and a child will love and accept you."

I grinned. "I've heard that a few times before. You know, being out here in this cocoon-type environment and having people program me to do all the right things, like eat what's healthy and go to sleep early — it makes what you say sound so simple. What happens when I leave here and go back in the real world?"

Catharina put her arms around me and gave me a incredibly warm hug. When she pulled away, she gazed at me with a serious expression on her face and said, " Clean all the confusion and doubt from your mind.

> **Understand your real purpose in life and you will not attract what and who is not good for you. Each day, look in the mirror and say to yourself, I am worthy, I am strong, I am loved."**

Then she suppressed a yawn and said, "and I am going to bed — after I check on Brookie to see if she is still spitting out choco- late cake."

It was my turn to smile. I thought about what Catharina had said and suddenly realized she had given me the answer behind the woman. For weeks I had studied her, envied her and wondered what her secret was. Now I knew. She was in harmony with herself and God, and in love with life.

Our final day at the Ashram had arrived. I was putting behind me the toughest, most worthwhile weeks of my life. When I put on my 'street clothes,' I was overjoyed at how loose they fit. And what a shame no one would notice my vibrant complexion beneath my make-up. Even my eyes sparkled. It seemed all the women had an aura of good health and serenity about them.

Catharina waited out in front of the main house to give us hugs. When it came time for mine, she grinned and said, "You did it, Donna. Good girl. You are beautiful. I see an inner strength you didn't have when you arrived."

"Thank you," I said, heartened by her words. "But, I couldn't have done it without you, Catharina."

She threw up her hands. "No, I didn't do it. You did. I was only your guide."

I smiled and said, "My mentor."

"Ja. One of those."

Before I got into the car, I took a final look at the grounds, the meditation dome and the main house. I gazed past the open door leading to the main room. Only the last line of the wooden sign was visible over the fireplace. I smiled knowingly at my assignment. It said *Be*.

✈ ✈ ✈

I walked into my apartment already missing the Ashram. When I heard a recent message from George on my voice-mail, my blue mood lifted.

"Hi Partner. I'm only in town until Monday. Where are you? Call me when you get in."

I immediately dialed the number of the hotel he was staying at. When I heard him answer, I said, "Hi, George, it's me."

"Good. Good. I was waiting to hear from you," he said.

"How did you know I would call?"

"Donna, *you know when you know.* How about getting together for our usual six o'clock breakfast tomorrow morning?"

Ashram time, I thought. "Sure, that's fine, George," I said, without my customary complaining.

After a long pause, George said, "Okay — great."

"And George, since your hotel is only eight blocks from my apartment, I'll just jog down and meet you."

"You? Jog? At six o'clock in the morning?"

I laughed and said, "I know that's hard for you to understand, but I just had the most incredible experience at the Ashram Retreat and well — never mind. I'll tell you all about it in the morning."

Dressed in sneakers and sweats, I jogged to the hotel beneath the fiery glow of a crimson sunrise.

After a big hug in the coffee shop, George stood back to observe me and said, "You look wonderful. What have you done to yourself?"

"That's what I need to tell you," I said grinning. "I always thought wonderful was only on the outside. I discovered from Catharina, at the Ashram, that wonderful happens on the inside. And I went helicopter skiing and met the most remarkable man named Raimund. Be proud of me, George." I said. "I'm healing and I'm growing."

"Oh boy, let's order some food first," George said with a chuckle. "Something tells me it's going to be one of *those* conversations." We sat down at a table by the window. When the waitress came, George asked for two coffees. He arched his brows in disbelief when I switched my coffee to herbal tea instead.

George squinted over his plate of ham and eggs and made a face at my fruit and Granola. He said, "You know, there is something different going on with you."

"George, you won't believe what I tell you about Catharina and Raimund. They're from totally different parts of the world and one's a woman and the other's a man — you probably figured that out — and they both think so much alike."

He chewed a piece of ham and said,

> **"Truth is truth. It doesn't matter who you hear it from, or where you find it."**

I explained my daily routine at the Ashram and said, "I hated the place when I first got there and loved the place when it was time to leave."

George looked amused. "I would have hated it at the beginning and hated it at the end."

"Well, I guess it's not for everyone," I said. "The more I learned about loving and accepting myself, the easier each day became. It was sort of like — a magical transformation." Up to this point, George had remained pretty quiet and had let me ramble on. "So, what do you think about all this?" I asked him.

He pushed his empty plate aside and fished out his pipe and tobacco pouch. "It's funny how you find those feelings and those answers when you least expect it. You become familiar in unfamiliar territory. It's a real good part of life."

I described how different Cliff and Raimund were. "I think I was so impressed by Raimund because for the first time, I had an honest relationship with a man my age. He taught me not to worry about what other people think, to get in touch with nature and to develop my spiritual wisdom. But the real revelation, George — I spoke openly to Catharina about my childhood fears. You and I have talked for hours about my family. Until the Ashram, you were the only person I shared my family secrets with. I guess I'd call Catharina and Raimund honest-to-goodness mentors. Am I right?"

"You bet. Mentors are guides to help you fulfill your potential and they appear when they're meant to. *When the student is ready the teacher arrives.* Those times when you were headstrong and afraid of change blocked the way for mentors to enter your life. Now, you've opened yourself to growth, and knowledge and they're helping you heal."

I sighed over my next question. "Will there ever come a time when I totally shed my past?"

George paused from packing tobacco into his pipe. "It's possible. Most folks don't admit hanging on to the past is a weakness. It takes a lot of work to put the past where it belongs. To imagine a new beginning without the old can be pretty scary, but when you understand the lesson, it enriches your life.

> **Live in the moment and glimpse the future.**

Be happy. Don't miss the sunsets and the walks along the beach," he chuckled, "and your fancy ice-cream cones." He gave me his little sideways squint. "What did you learn from Catharina and Raimund about *the moment?*"

"Well," I said between munches, "with Catharina, my world became the moment. I had more awareness. I felt my strength, touched nature and my mind and body were in tune — one foot in front of the other. With Raimund, it was exhausting, exhilarating and I needed to conquer the mountain — and my fears. I didn't have time to think of anything else. Because I achieved all those things, I feel so positive about myself."

George smiled and said, "You were given circumstances that gave you wonderful lessons. There are no accidents, everything happens for a reason and your learning lessons help you understand your inner wisdom.

> ## It's the inner wisdom and persistence that gives you truth."

"I've already been hard at work persisting." I laughed and said, "I forgot to tell you, George, my landlord evicted all the tenants from our little two-story colonial building up the street, right here in Westwood. He gave us all thirty days to move out. There's senior citizens and college students living in the building and we're all in the same dilemma. And get this, he's going to build a big high-rise building in its place."

"That's too bad. Where will you go?" George asked.

"I've been looking, but I can't find anything affordable. So, I rallied all the tenants together and we fought the eviction."

"Hey, that's good," George said. "Sounds like you took the wind out of your landlord's skyscraper plans."

"He wouldn't even listen to me when I told him we needed at least sixty days. Some of older the tenants have lived there for years. It's their home and it just wasn't — ."

"It wasn't fair," George finished. "He wasn't honorable. He wasn't kind."

"Exactly." George's words had formed an impression and I glanced across the table at him. "It has to do with people's values, doesn't it?"

He nodded. "Yup, and respect for people."

"You want to hear the happy ending?" I asked, and kept talking without waiting for an answer. "We all banded together and got a six months extension — and that's not all. Certain people, I won't name names, had our building declared a historical landmark and the owner had to find another lot to move it on before he could build his high-rise." I laughed hilariously, until tears streamed down my face. "I don't think he likes me. The last thing he said to me was, please don't move into another of my buildings. Then — would you believe he offered me a job in his company."

George grinned, held out his hands, palms up. "Donna, I think I'll just stay your friend, but I would be proud to wear your shoes, Partner."

I sighed. "Seriously, George, I can't find another area I want to live in and my career is doing just so-so. Because of what's gone on these last months, I've made a decision. I want to move to the mountains in Northern California. I've been there with my father and brother and I love it. It means I'll have to give up acting and find a new career. It's change and it's scary. But how do you think I'll earn my living?"

George tucked his tobacco pouch in his pocket and held his unlit pipe in his hand. He took a deep breath and his eyes glazed over with a faraway look. After a while, he turned to me and said, "You're going to talk."

"I meant, what am I going to do for a career?"

"What do you do best?"

"Huh?"

"Talk. That's what you do best and it's going to be your new career." He glanced at his watch and pushed back his chair. "I have an eight o'clock meeting and I'll explain some other time."

"Promise?"

"I promise."

I picked up the check and said, "I really have changed. For once, George, breakfast is on me."

JOURNAL
The Power of Mentors

I was resistant to change until the plane crash. After that, I was vulnerable, searching and open. I wanted guidance and I needed to ask questions to learn answers. Just as George predicted, when the time was right the mentors came into my life. And as I think back, they were from all walks of life. There was Catharina, the drill sergeant and saint and Raimund, the ski guide who had so much perception and understanding of life. And, of course, my dear, wise friend George. They all shared the common ground of wisdom. The mentors who guided and supported me live in the moment. Until now, I didn't really understand that outlook. I wound up missing today because I kept on hoping the next day would bring what I wanted.

I was caught up in the give me, take me, show me, buy me Hollywood lifestyle. The happiness it brought was short lived. The best healing time for me was the simple lasting joy I got from nature: standing on a mountain top and gazing down at the dazzling white powder, fresh cold air on my face and the freedom of skiing; hiking up a dirt mountain, building endurance, the sensation of accomplishment; the peace of meditation and cleansing from the inside out. Whoever thought I'd trade my sack of brownies for fruit, yogurt and water?

Universe, I understand how important it is to keep healing, but the reality is I have to get back to work and create a living for myself. When I worked with famous stars like Tim Reed, Robin Williams, John Ritter and Richard Pryor, I just read lines. I wasn't putting me into my acting. I have a strong intuitive feeling I need to move away from Los Angeles and into a new career. And now is the time for me to make a change. So, I ask these questions: Since I feel a career in Hollywood is no longer right for me, how do I determine the work I will love and how will I know it will be right for me? I've had many mentors in my life, but I never understood they were there to help me grow. Now I'm thankful and feel blessed to have them in my life. I've listened to their wisdom and claim the knowledge I have received from them.

> **The powers of mentors guide
> and heal with wisdom.**

Manifest Your Passion

The pilot announced our landing in Honolulu. I adjusted my
seat upwards and tightened my
seatbelt. Sudden turbulence jostled the plane and I gripped the
armrests. Fear spun wildly through my mind and my heart raced.
The haunting vision flashed before me: an aircraft on fire, people
burning and screaming in pain and fright, stunned survivors sitting in huddles. Seconds dragged before I could tear my hands
away from the armrests and gain control over myself.

Over the past five years, my anxiety attacks had occurred less
frequently, but I was never forewarned when the next would happen. I took deep breaths to calm myself and glanced out the right
window. We were swooping down over the brilliant blues of the

Oahu coast. I looked down on Diamond Head and the sight of beckoning palm trees and waves breaking on the white sandy beach transported me back to the nostalgic magic of the island. I was coming home.

I felt a slight jolt on touch-down and smiled to myself as the aircraft made a perfect landing. Coming down the ramp, over the odor of jet fuel, I smelled the sweet scent of Plumeria and caught the warm, tropical sea breeze like silk against my face.

By the time the taxi had dropped me off at my hotel in Waikiki, I'd pinched myself several times. More than anything, I'd wanted to return to Hawaii. When I first came to the islands, I was a starving college student who sold pots and pans to pay my tuition at the University of Hawaii. I had no money and lived on rice, pineapple, guava and coconuts. I ended up becoming Miss Hawaii, living at the Colony Surf on the water at Diamond Head and becoming a top sales person. It was a five year period of slow progress for me — a time when I worked hard and actually carved out a successful life for myself. For me, Hawaii was an enchanted spot. It bolstered my confidence like nowhere else.

I had just enough time to check into my room and freshen up before I was due to meet my former cookware boss, Chuck Smart, a man whose last name brought a smile to my lips. Maybe that's why I listened to him, because he really was smart. I dressed casually in white pants and a sleeveless blue shell and walked the short distance to an old favorite restaurant, the Tahitian Lanai. I loved the atmosphere of grass hut dining and tables arranged around the swimming pool. Chuck saw me right away and flagged me over. One would have to be sightless to overlook the big, powerfully built man. He had chiseled features, dark hair and chestnut eyes that brimmed with character. I was excited to see him again.

"How's my Dynamite Donna doing," he asked, his big arms encircling me in a hug.

I gave him a broad smile. "Great, Chuck. And how is the king of pots and pans doing?"

He grinned. "Well, you gotta eat, so you gotta cook. Pots and pans are doing super."

He took my arm and steered me into one of the little Tahitian huts. I said, "I'm impressed, Chuck. The huts are reserved way ahead of time."

He tossed me one of his famous winks. "I reserved this hut especially for Miss Hawaii."

Dressed in her long floral muumuu, the waitress stopped at our table to take our orders. After she left, I smiled across the table at Chuck thinking how tan and healthy he looked. I always loved seeing him. He was an easy conversationalist, generous with his advice and really understood people. Our drinks arrived with a tray of appetizers the Hawaiians call poo-poo's and as we nibbled Chuck said, "You moved from L.A., so where are you now?"

"Chuck, more like where do I start?" I sighed heavily. "I've been through massive change since giving up Hawaii for Hollywood. My apartment building in Los Angeles was sold from under me and I've since moved to the high Sierras. You know, famous for blustery winters, unpredictable weather and magnificent Lake Tahoe."

Chuck raised one dark, fly-away brow. "Why there? I thought you were a warm weather gal."

"I still like warm weather, but I love to ski. When I was in junior high, I attended the 1960 Olympics at Squaw Valley with my father and brother. I adored it there. I visited a little church with stained glass windows and prayed I could someday live in Tahoe. Now, twenty years later, I'm living in that very same safe, healing place. I actually made my decision to move on the exact two year anniversary date of the plane crash."

Chuck nodded. "Dream it and it'll happen."

"That's exactly why I'm here," I said. "I have a dream and I need to make it happen."

"Okay, Donna —let's hear it."

I paused to figure out where to begin. After a moment I said, "I came to Hawaii to speak at a conference. I can speak just fine; however, I know nothing about running my own business. I don't have much money, but I have to start somewhere. Fact is, I'm living in my brother's house overlooking Lake Tahoe in Squaw Valley. Thirteen ski-happy people, dead poor, in the same house." I could see Chuck was restraining one of his boisterous laughs. "Believe me, I've done my share of serving cocktails just to survive." I leveled my index finger at my head. "Me, who doesn't know a gimlet from a martini. I kept putting olives in drinks that needed cherries." I looked around at the other tables and said, "The only way I know cocktails in Hawaii is if they're on fire or have umbrellas floating on top."

Chuck laughed. "You never were much for the hard stuff," he said.

"Anyhow, I started out working in Reno, Nevada, with young kids who wanted to do commercials. That's the closest city to Tahoe. Then the parents came to me and asked how I motivated the kids to learn. Well, one thing led to another and they asked me to speak for small groups and from there, I went on to speak for large companies. I spoke about changing your attitude and at the end of the speech, touched on the crash and how I had to change my attitude to survive. Afterwards, people would come up to me and asked a lot of questions about the plane crash and how my life had changed. Like I said, Chuck, I can do the talking, and I love it, but I don't understand the business end of it very well. I don't know how to set it up, or how to run it. That's where you come in. You ran a business and an entire crew of people. I need your expert advice."

Chuck leaned in close and his dark brows merged at the bridge of his nose. I remembered that same intense look when he wanted to make a point at our cookware meetings. "Let's start off with when you first came to work for me," he said. "You were a penniless college student — you had to pay fifteen dollars for a bond to sell pots and pans — and your check bounced."

I nodded. "I was broke."

"Donna, did you sell any cookware that first month?"

"Your memory is too good, Chuck. No. I didn't sell any cookware."

"Why not"

I sighed and said, "I thought I was too good to knock on doors and sell pots and pans. I didn't like doing it and my friends said it was a stupid job. I felt my parents should be paying for all my education, but they weren't. I had a bad attitude, so I — I didn't sell any cookware." I turned away from Chuck's searching eyes. "And yes, you did what any boss would do. You fired me."

After a moment, Chuck said, "I did what I had to do."

"I know. But, remember, I came back to talk to you later that day and cried and pleaded to get my job back." I took a deep breath and smiled my appreciation. "Thanks, Chuck, for giving me another shot at it."

He nodded. "I knew you had it in you all along, kid. You just needed a little direction, and an attitude adjustment."

"I sure did. After you hired me back, I remember you went out with me and taught me how to sell. Having you there boosted my confidence and. . . ."

"Hang on a minute. Let's not get ahead of ourselves," Chuck said and tossed me a look. "That day when you came back after I fired you, what changed your mind about selling cookware?"

"I had to. I didn't have any money."

Chuck nodded. "I'd say, that's a cool reason. At first, you listened to other people who weren't thinking of your best interest. That happens in any business. You just had to learn to stop listening to bad advice. *It's you* who decides who to listen to and who not to listen to. "

I flashed him a questioning look.

"Donna, you'll get all kinds of advice. Pay close attention to who is giving you advice, and let your gut tell you if this person is an achiever and has a good track record. Okay. What happened to you then?"

"I lived and breathed selling cookware until I became thirteenth in the United States in sales. Not bad for a person who got fired. I'll never forget I won a full scholarship to college and that beats paying."

"That's right. It was a perfect job for you at the time. After awhile, you kicked back, enjoyed. You had a real passion for what you did. You liked running a crew of people, coming to meetings and getting bonuses — and being late for meetings because you were surfing." I rolled my eyes. "What else spurred you on?" Chuck asked, his enthusiasm bubbling up.

"I found fulfillment. I enjoyed the people, the recognition and I really believed in the product."

"Oh yeah. You bet! You have to believe in what you're doing."

"And I really believe I want to keep speaking, Chuck, but how do I keep it going? I'm starting from nothing. I don't have pots and pans to sell. I just have me."

Chuck's eyes widened. "Oh? So what's wrong with you? You have to believe in yourself, Donna. Back in those days, I saw the potential in you, but you didn't." He paused and inhaled deeply. "Let me give you a few more tips to help you figure it out. Remember when I had you write out goals predicting how much cookware you would sell each week?"

"Yes, of course. I couldn't forget being scared I wouldn't make my own goals."

"Why don't you do that now? Set your time frames and see where you want to be — a month, three months, six months, a year from now. What kind of lifestyle do you want? How much money do you want to make? How do you want to give back to other people? And don't forget to make time for the fun things. Then, get organized. If you're working for yourself, you have to set guidelines and stick by them. Set a schedule. What time do you get up? When do you start work? How many calls will you make and don't forget to follow-up. Just like you did with pots and pans."

"Okay. What else?" I asked, excited from what I was hearing.

Chuck smiled. "When people work for themselves, the greatest cause of failure is not managing time. Don't let procrastination steal your time. You be in charge and set those priorities. You know how this works. Think back to when you had a Christmas Eve deadline in the company contest to earn your scholarship and all you needed was one more sale.

"Oh — yes. I remember. I called you on Christmas Eve to say I was banging on doors and getting turned down right and left. I was afraid I wouldn't make it.

"That's right. Then, you ran into an R&R couple from Vietnam and the guy said, I just got in, haven't bought my wife anything for Christmas and cookware is exactly what she needs. You called me and I asked you. . . ."

I interrupted. "You asked me what I was doing selling cookware on Christmas Eve. Actually, I was supposed to go to a luau with my friends, but I couldn't go because I felt getting my scholarship was more important than going out with my friends. I had worked for days getting that last sale and nothing happened."

Chuck laughed. "That's what I call managing your time. You prioritized, got the sale, made the deadline and won your scholarship. You learned it paid to keep your eye on the target."

I took a sip of juice and said, "Uh-huh. And he was really cute too."

"Who?"

"My date. I caught up with him later at the luau." I got a look. "Chuck, luau's are the best."

He laughed. "Right. So, you made time for fun too. You do know how to prioritize, Dynamite Donna. And you've got some work ahead of you. Figure out your goals, get organized and be persistent." Chuck grinned and said, "I'm a risk taker and a betting man, and I'd bet on you."

He drove me to my hotel as darkness closed in on the pinkish glow of the sunset. I, thanked him for all his great advice and told him how wonderful it was to see him again.

Later that night, back in my room, I thought more about our conversation. I had never considered Chuck my mentor, but he'd had a powerful impact on me and my future. He taught me to provide for myself, how to keep the momentum going and how to be passionate about what I wanted.

The next morning I woke up at dawn. I dressed in shorts, rented a bicycle and headed for the peaceful little refuge I shared with no one. The ride to Diamond Head was uplifting and I could feel my body rebounding to the vigorous up and down hill workout. When I caught sight of my favorite sitting rock, I jumped off my bike and leaned it against a palm tree. This was where I came to align myself with nature. I sat down and took a few moments to relax. Then I closed my eyes and began to meditate. The sound of breaking waves and the warm sun on my back had a calming effect.

I opened my eyes to a cluster of surfers paddling out to catch their first waves of the day. I watched for hours, thinking back to my college days when, at sunrise, I would be out riding the waves. I'd surf all morning and quit in barely enough time to attend my cookware meetings. It wasn't unusual for me to show up with wet hair and bare feet. I had forgotten how incredible it was to be that much in touch with water. I wanted to feel that alive once more. I wanted to surf again. But it would have to wait. I had a luncheon date.

I peddled back to the hotel and changed into a sleeveless cotton dress. It was an easy walk from Waikiki to the Ala Moana

Shopping Center. I passed the pond of carp and the little book-store where Dr. Bob took me to select self-help books. The locals referred to him as Dr. Gibson, but to me he was always Dr. Bob.

After winning the title of Miss Hawaii, I needed my teeth capped and I was referred to Dr. Bob Gibson. His reputation was that of the most popular, brilliant and expensive dentist on the island. I liked him right away. He was a philanthropist at heart, an aloha friendly man with a black mustache and an engaging stutter. I remember my first visit well. I settled back in his chair and opened my mouth and he prodded and poked and said, Uh-huh..we'll move this...get the right color...redo those four teeth...oh, yes...perfect! Yuh-yuh-yuh you will be marvelous when we're da-da done."

When his receptionist added up the cost for all my improve-ments, I said, "Huh-huh-how much?" I thought the price outra-geous, but I returned every week for three months, with my cook-ware proceeds, to pay his bill. And each week Dr. Bob would give me a different self-help book to read. During the following visit, busy as he was, he always took the time to discuss the book with me. My teeth turned out gorgeous, the job of a real perfectionist. What I didn't know at the time was that he was not only chang-ing my outside appearance, but improving me from the inside out. That was Dr. Bob's greatest gift to me.

The Ala Moana Professional Building was right next door to the shopping center. I took the elevator to the top floor where the revolving restaurant offered diners a great view of Honolulu. I asked for Dr. Bob's booth and there he was, punctual as ever, already waiting.

When I sat down, he covered my hand with his and said, "Wonderful to see you, Donna. I only have a short time, but I took the liberty of ordering a papaya lunch for us."

I grinned and exclaimed, "I love papaya."

We made small talk and caught up on the news during lunch. After we had finished eating, Dr. Bob pushed his plate away and became serious. "When you ca-ca-called me a few days ago, Donna, you said it was absolutely important we meet. What's all this about?"

"Dr. Bob, I'm here in Hawaii to do a speech for a group of top executives. I'm the new kid in the speaking profession. I remember when you gave me all those positive thinking books and how reading them changed my life. That's what I want to do when I speak. I want to change people's lives. I met with my former boss last night and have a much better idea of how to organize and stay focused, but I don't know where to start with the business end. Do I hire an accountant or a secretary?" I grinned and said, "If I have to hire both, I'm in big trouble."

Dr. Bob laughed and said, "I understand. I'm going to give you my two pearls of wisdom. First, no matter how many people you speak before, keep taking classes, attend seminars, read books, listen to self-help tapes and watch videos that help you grow. Invest in yourself, Donna. Stretch your mind. There is no limit to self improvement. You are who you think you are." He sat back and sighed. "and the second little pearl — always go to the top."

I nodded. "I understand about the books and all that, but what do you mean by 'the go to the top'?"

Dr. Bob furrowed his brow for a moment and said, "When you need help with accounting, brochures, or you're searching out coaching, do the research. Go to the ta-ta-top people and ask for guidance because that's where you want to position yourself — at the top. Those are my two pearls of wisdom." He glanced at his watch. "Donna, I have a patient waiting to get his teeth fixed. Gotta get back da-da-down to my office."

"Dr. Bob," I murmured, "you don't fix teeth, you fix lives."

He chuckled, "Well, a little of both." He reached down on the seat and handed me a book. "Just saw this in the bookstore and thought you might like it."

I grinned when I saw the cover. "Oh perfect! It's the one I saw in the window on the way over here."

"By the way, there's a phone message tucked inside the cover. Someone called my office looking for you. Seems every time your name gets in the Who's Who column in the newspaper, people start calling me to look for you."

I smiled and said, "Dr. Bob, thanks for the book and for being my answering service. People seem to know I always see you when I come to Hawaii."

I said good-by to Dr. Bob and unfolded the message. I was delighted to learn it was from George and read:

I'm overdue for one of those flaming volcano drinks. I'll be in Hawaii tonight. Join me at the Hilton Hawaiian Village at eight o'clock.

I thought, George in Hawaii. Wow! And I'll even have time to go surfing before I meet with him.

✈ ✈ ✈

The waves at Diamond Head were breaking at about three feet. I paddled out on a friend's borrowed surfboard trying to connect with the water. Surfing requires balance and timing, and I had to get my sea legs back. A lot of time had passed since I rode the board with the locals and I hoped I still had the competence to perform. The thought of riding the face of a breaking wave had me exploding with excitement. An unexpected wave pressed me into action. I could tell my timing was off. I gasped, my body tightened. There was no time to flip the board on top of me and wrap my feet around it. Had I done so, I would have waited beneath the water for the wave to break over me, then flip the board back up and paddle out. But, I had ignored the basics. The wave battered me as if trying to wash me from the world. I lost the surfboard and had to swim back to the beach. My arms were trembling from exhaustion by the time I carried the board back into the water.

The next try, I got about half way out to the breaking area when another wave came at me. I lost the board. After that, I wiped out time and again. My arms were numb and I could feel the blazing sun scorch my back. This was not what I expected. Instead of riding the waves to shore, the waves slammed me and tossed me around before I even got near the breaking point.

I don't know why I kept paddling back out, maybe just plain bullheadness. I finally made it past the breaking point and sat on the surfboard waiting for the wave I could master. But, hard as I tried, I missed five waves. Embarrassed, I glanced around me at the sun-bronzed local surfers, and sensed their mocking stares and astonished silence. I was the only 'hollie,' pale-faced, red haired female out there. I could only wonder why I kept flopping around with a pack of finely synchronized surfers who rode the waves like dolphins. Then, I noticed one of the locals break away from the line and paddle over to me.

He smiled and said, "Ey — rough day?"

"Believe it or not," I said all flustered, "I used to surf all the time, but I've been away for a couple of years." Then, I thought to myself, actually a lot more than a couple.

He nodded. "Hmmm. Too anxious. Kick back. Get one with wave."

"You're right." I smiled, thinking how long it had been since I'd heard the local pigeon. "That's it. I'm just too anxious."

"Ey. Loosen up. You live here?"

"No, not any more. I graduated from the University."

"Ey. You gonna be here awhile — maybe surf again?"

"I'm here for a couple of days. I might come out again. I could use the practice."

He smiled and winked. "See you tomorrow. We get together."

Just then, the surfer swivelled his head and said, "Ey. That's your wave. You catch it."

I inhaled and exhaled a few times. When the wave crested, I caught it, past the point of breakage as it peaked and before it passed beneath me. Ecstatic, I stood up on the board, and I rode it all the way to shore. The perfect wave had found me and I had caught it. My failures were lessons and a reminder to not force nature, but respect it.

I rode the waves until I wore myself out. As I sat waiting for my last wave of the day, I glanced over at the line of surfers and this time the locals gave me a 'thumb's up.'

My newfound friend paddled over and said, "Ey. You no talk story. You really surf."

I grinned. "Yes, I can. But, it sure helps to have a little advice from a local."

By the time I got back to my hotel, I felt exhilarated, but exhausted. I left a message for George telling him I would meet him at eight. Then, I took a shower and fell asleep.

✈ ✈ ✈

When I arrived at the Hilton, I went directly to the outside lounge area to find George. I scanned the faces for a few seconds and it wasn't long before I heard, "Hey partner!" I turned and there he was, sitting at a table beneath the Tiki torches, dressed in a colorful Hawaiian shirt and smoking his pipe.

He beckoned to me and said, "Get over here. I need to order my volcano drink right now, before it erupts."

I shook my head and laughed. I hugged George, sat down and promptly asked, "What on earth are you doing in Hawaii? What a great surprise!"

Before George could answer, the waiter came for our orders. After he left, George said, "I'm here because I got a call from a client in Honolulu who needed me. The only way to knock some sense into him and give him some help was to get right over to Hawaii. I got the first flight out and here I am. I remembered you said you'd be here about now, so I just called Dr. Gibson."

"This is great, because it's been so long since I've seen you and here we are back in Hawaii where it all began. Do you remember. . . . ?

George laughed. "Donna, I don't even have my drink yet and you're starting."

Cherry pipe smoke spiraled above George's head and scented the air around us. "But I have something important to tell you, " I said. "When I asked you what kind of work I would do, you said, "You're going to talk. Well, you were right on. I'm actually talking — for a living."

Our drinks arrived. George took a sip of his flaming concoction, sighed and sat back. "About what you just said. It's not only that you're making a living, or even making a career for yourself. You told me the last time we spoke, you were talking for a purpose and that you want to help people."

"And am I glad you're here in Hawaii right now," I said. I took a job to speak at a large conference — executives from all over the world. I'm the keynote speaker — you know, I kick things off."

George sipped his drink and tossed me a questioning look. "That's good. What are you going to talk about?"

"About the plane crash, how to handle changes and challenges. I've really prepared, did my research, studied all my notes, and yet, it seems my message is almost too simple — maybe even inadequate. George, how can my story of surviving a plane crash change lives? I'm afraid it's not important enough." No sooner had I said it than I realized I'd used the fear word. I could already tell by George's silence he was revving up to cancel my trepidations.

He puffed and said, "Let's go back to basics, Donna. Why do you think these people are going to come and hear you speak?"

"I don't have a clue," I said stubbornly.

"Oh, yes you do. You overcame massive fear when you faced death and almost died in the accident. Everyone in the human race has fears. Doesn't matter how important you are, or how much money you have. What you're going to speak about is a real life experience. Tell them what you learned, how important life is, and how you overcame fear to take the witness stand and fight for safety regulations." George stared out at the ash orange and plum colored sunset. Several seconds later he said, "You got the steak from the plane crash and the sizzle from the Hollywood years. So, when you speak, you've got steak and sizzle and they'll listen. But even more than that, Donna, don't forget to tell those people how they can make changes to enjoy a better life. Give them some steps so they can find purpose and happiness before it's their time to meet their maker."

I nodded. "I know you're right and I get your point, George, but it still sounds too simple — too hokey."

"It's not hokey at all. See, you're connecting with them, creating new understanding. People are the same world over. Humanity has the same hopes, loves, expectations, fears. You're bringing all that to light. Remember when I said you were born to talk? That's how you help people help themselves — through your talking. It's what you claim for yourself — what you manifest."

I knew about manifesting material things, but now I was confused again. "Manifesting my speaking?" I asked. "How the heck do I do that?"

George, deep in thought, flared a match and re-lit his pipe. "I've got a little recipe I put together to help people understand what manifestation is. Once you really understand it, you can put it into action and some darn good things can happen."

"You've got me going, George. I want to hear this recipe."

He chuckled. "Okay. Let's say you want something real bad. You put the five A's to work for you.

"The five A's?" I asked.

"Those are the ingredients. Of course you have to manifest them in the right order — kind of like making a cake. Are you ready to listen?"

I rolled my eyes. "George...."

He held up his index finger and said,

First, *acknowledge* what it is you want. Then, you *accept* it as yours, like you already have it. Now, you have to take some *action* to make it happen. Then, you ease back a little and *ask if what you want is for your highest good*. Here's the good part. You may not have what you want yet, but you still give *appreciation* that the Universe is providing for you. Sometimes what you ask for happens right away and sometimes it takes awhile. Are you getting it?"

"Well, let's see if I understand this. You're telling me I can manifest the right thing to say to people. I'll know inside of me that what I'm saying is what they want to hear? George, just how am I going to pull that one off?"

"Donna, think about the speeches you've given. Anything special happen?"

I smiled briefly. "Yes. Sometimes after I give a speech, a person in the audience will come up to me and say, "I just wanted you to know, you were talking to me.""

"Good. And that's what your purpose is. To help one person at a time. It's in their eyes, Donna. When you look out in the audience and you speak the universal language of truth, you'll see understanding in the eyes." He fluttered his hand. "And not everyone is going to like everything you say. Don't let that put you in a tailspin. When people are ready to change, they'll learn. You were meant to help people help themselves.

When people get sick and tired of being sick and tired, they'll change."

I sat straight up. "I remember those exact words coming to me in the crash."

"That's right, Donna. Now those folks who listen are going to do the work, but the guidance and wisdom is all in your story."

"Then, how can I be positive what I say is what people need to hear?"

"*You'll know when you know.*"

I grinned. "You've been saying that to me for years, George."

"I can't make it any easier to understand than that, Donna."

"I have a headache just thinking about tomorrow," I said while pressing a hand to my forehead.

"That's because you're judging yourself. Learn your skills and be prepared. But remember, polish and perfection is only a part of your presentation. If you speak from your heart and your insight, you'll help put people on the path to do their own work"

"You're sure — people really want to hear what I have to say?"

"Yup."

I grinned and said, "I'm going to keep practicing and I'm not sure how well I'll do, but I promise to give it my best shot."

"Now you're cooking. Each time you speak, you'll get a little better at it."

"Right, George." I chuckled. Maybe I should be drinking the volcano drink tonight instead of the fruit juice."

"You stay on the juice," George said, his face crinkling up in a huge smile. You have to give a speech tomorrow morning. By the way, where are you doing your talking?"

"In the main ballroom at the Sheraton Hotel, here in Waikiki."

"Good." He waved for the check and said, "We'd better call it a night. You need your rest. Just remember what I said, and don't worry. Build on your passion and what you love to do. And I can say, you love to talk.

> Once you do what you
> love and do it with passion,
> it becomes your success."

By the time I had returned to my hotel, my headache had disappeared. I read over my speech, made some minor changes and went to bed. I awoke at four in the morning with a case of the jitters and reviewed my speech until my brain was on overload. I didn't sleep much after that.

I arrived at the hotel ballroom early the next morning. I was speaking to my largest audience yet. Even as people poured into reception area to chat with one another over Danish and coffee, I still found it hard to believe they had come to hear me speak. I walked to the lobby, took some deep breaths and composed myself. One voice inside me was saying, "I couldn't do it." The other was saying "It's your time."

After I returned to the ballroom and stepped up to the stage, the emcee signaled me to stand behind the curtain. I squeezed out every morsel of energy to stay centered as I waited through ten agonizing minutes of the emcee giving thanks and introductions. I shook my arms to ease stress. I coughed and swallowed several times to relieve dry throat. When it finally came time to introduce me, the emcee announced:

"Let me set the scene. It's March 1, 1978. Our speaker is on her way from Los Angeles to Honolulu to emcee the Miss Hawaii pageant. That day changed her life forever."

I felt my insides plummet as the room went dark and my plane crash reenactment sound effects went into action. I shuddered through each second of the dramatic introduction. I was being devoured by flames. The wailing of ambulance sirens tightened my stomach. I gasped for breath and then, I heard the soothing words:

> "Do you love yourself? Do you have a good relationship with your family and friends? Are you living your goals and dreams? If you die today, have you left this planet a better place for being here?"

The audio tape wound to a finish and I heard my voice scream out, "I want to live!" Then, I walked to the center stage and said, "I'm Donna Hartley. I'm alive and loving life, but answer these two questions: *Are you really alive and are you loving your life?*"

The applause was spontaneous and heartwarming. I felt great and the fears were gone. As I smiled and glimpsed the faces of my audience, I glanced toward the back of the room. I was astonished to see the familiar, portly figure of George. He'd come to give me support. His compassion and guidance had enabled me to trust in myself and to live in this moment. He raised his arms up and clasped his hands together in a winning salute. Then he turned and disappeared through the double doors.

JOURNAL
Manifest Your Passion

I'm sitting here on the lanai overlooking the ocean, writing by candlelight beneath a huge and beautiful moon. This visit to Hawaii has been deeply satisfying and I mastered my personal doubts. Surfing put me back in touch with the ocean and served to focus and align myself. Today I stood on stage and spoke the words to help people help themselves. I must admit, I was afraid. I realize now I was judging myself. Once I walked on the stage and began speaking, the fear disappeared. The question I read in the eyes of the audience was, *"Why am I here and what is the purpose of my life?"* I discovered they really wanted to hear a message of hope, just like I wanted a sign in the plane crash.

Speaking is fulfilling and gives my life purpose. Of course, since I'm just launching my career, I have financial concerns and anxiety about the next time I appear on stage. Those are things I can conquer. What I really love is the joy in serving other people and guiding them to rise beyond their own expectations.

I've been so blessed to have mentors that have enhanced my life with incredible knowledge. Seeing Chuck was like old times again. And dear Dr. Bob with his book in hand. And George, who is always there for me, patiently droning out his wisdom. As I think about what he said, I actually have manifested many things in my life. I just need a little more practice to understand how the five A's work — and to remember them: *Acknowledge* what it is I want. *Accept* it as mine, like I already have it. Take *action* to make it happen. Ease back and *ask if what I want is for my highest good.* Give *appreciation* that the Universe is providing for me.

My question to the Universe is: *Can I apply manifestation to all levels of my life and does it happen right away?* I sense the word 'action' popping into my mind. I don't know exactly what that means, but it's so loud and clear that I feel positive 'action' is the answer to my question. I'm just not sure what role it will play in manifestation.

Universe, I'm so thankful I conquered my fear today and that as a speaker, I gave something that mattered to someone. It was an indescribable feeling when people came up to me and said my information was important to them. I asked my audience today what I ask myself everyday:

> **Do you love yourself? Do you have a good relationship with your family and friends? Are you living your goals and dreams? If you die today, have you left this planet a better place for being here?**

Action Creates Attraction

My fortieth birthday hit me like a truck-load of con-crete. Ten years since the crash and I was stuck trying to get my life together. Still single — outlook grim. Didn't have a child — outlook grim. And I didn't own a house — now *that* I could change. I figured out how much rent I had paid over the last twenty-two years, and that convinced me I had to buy a house — now.

I'd started my business on a shoe string and every cent I had made went right back into it. When I saw a commercial for a "Nothing Down Real Estate Seminar," it got my attention. I contacted the promoters and offered to trade a critique on the presenter's communication techniques for a free seminar. Sold!

The real estate experts advised, "Look at a bunch of houses, make a lot of offers and if the seller bites, go for a lease option — someone who will accept larger monthly payments in lieu of an immediate mortgage payoff."

It made sense to me and I took their suggestions. I spent all my time searching and fell in love with a house I couldn't live without. It was cozy and warm with beautiful blooming trees, oodles of windows and a view of Lake Tahoe. Joanne, who owned the house, was going through a divorce and moving out of the area. Perfect for my situation. It was all those little zeros at the end of the selling price that had me asking for divine guidance. In fact, it was a hundred thousand dollars more than I expected to pay.

I made my first offer: I'd move in, live in the house for eighteen months, pay double rent, and all that money would go toward the down payment. I thought it was a brilliant idea. The owner ripped up the offer. "I know this is the house for me," I said to Joanne. "It's meant to be mine and no one else will buy it." In hindsight, I shouldn't have been that blunt. I drove home thinking I'd really bungled the offer and that night I sobbed myself to sleep.

By the next morning, I made up my mind to stay optimistic and forge ahead. I went back and took pictures of the outside of the house and tacked them up throughout my rental unit. I actually envisioned myself living in the house.

The next month, I made another offer. The owner didn't rip it up, but neither did she acknowledge it. To achieve more leverage over myself, I mentally changed my address — as though I was already living in the house. Four weeks later, I made my third offer. Again, no word from the owner. I was so sure she would acquiesce, I purchased a sofa, love seat and chair for the living room.

After I made my fourth offer, I had convinced myself I'd get the key to the front door. The silence from the other end put me into a colossal depression. The owner had made it painfully clear she was not interested. Feeling vulnerable and powerless, I assumed I didn't have the necessary resources to buffer me against another setback. My belief system was eroding and I began thinking my friends were right when they said I was crazy to attempt buying a house with no money down. I still drove past the house, but I was overwhelmed by doubt, and I could no longer visualize myself living in it.

A few days after my last offer, I had just returned from a long walk in the mountains when I heard the phone ring. I ran to answer it and it was George.

He said, "You know, Partner, I've never been to Lake Tahoe." I heard his familiar chuckle across the line. "Next week seems a good time for me to visit."

His timing couldn't have been better. "George — how is it you always know when I'm having a crisis and need help?"

In his straight-talking Oklahoma accent, he said, "*You know when you know.*"

I couldn't help smiling. "You and your Georgeisms. You've been saying that to me forever. Come on now — tell me what that really means."

I heard a chuckle and he said, "Think about it. Nobody else has to tell you a thing. You don't have doubt. You just know that's the way it is. Like I know it's time for me to come to Tahoe."

✈ ✈ ✈

I arrived at the Reno airport late in the evening and George was already waiting outside. His eyes crinkled with a big smile and he rubbed his hands together saying, "It sure is cold up here. Feels ready to snow."

He was right. The next morning when I drove up to the lodge where George had booked a room, it was blowing snow everywhere. He sauntered outside, dressed for a blustery Tahoe day. He wore jeans, western boots, and a warm jacket, and I smelled the familiar aroma of his cherry tobacco.

The roads were slick and icy and I drove to the restaurant with more than a normal amount of caution. We found a table near a blazing fireplace and sat down. Scanning the menu, George said, "I'm having a big mountain breakfast, and from the looks of you, a pancake or two would stick to your bones. You're going to need some fuel if you're going to stack wood and take care of your house."

"George," I said dejectedly, "I've made four offers — I was so sure. You told me to stay positive. I did what you said, and I haven't heard a word from Joanne. I'm thinking it just won't happen for me."

George pushed his plate back and gave me one of his insightful looks. "It works like this Donna," he said, *The more powerful your vision, the more it demands of you.* And owning a house is a pretty powerful vision."

"I'm learning that the hard way. I always figured I couldn't afford my own place. Now that I've turned forty, I really want a house."

He held up his hand. "Wait just a minute. Let's back up now. Four offers you said. Why didn't the owner accept?"

"Because I made the offers with no money down. I was hoping she would take a lease option."

George's face registered surprise. "Well, Donna, I don't think if I were her, I'd take your terms either. I'd want some money."

"George, of course she'll get the money, but she won't get it all right now, because I have to go out and create it first. You know. We talked about how I work that backwards formula. When I have a dream, I don't let finances, timing, or obstacles stand in my way. I just go for it and I keep my eye on the objective — in this case, the house. I actually imagined I was living in it. I saw myself redecorating and furnishing it. And no matter how many times Joanne turned me down, I managed my fear and stuck to my plan." I stared into the fire feeling downhearted. "I do the backwards formula all the time and it usually works, but this time it didn't."

George sat back, a puzzled look on his face. After a moment, he said, "Tell me about this lease option? Explain how it works."

I filled in the details and George asked the questions.

"Is Joanne moving out of the area?"

"She's already gone and has the house rented out to tenants because it didn't sell."

"Why do you think she didn't accept your offer?"

"Because I just think Joanne wanted the traditional deal."

"Anyone else make an offer on it?"

"No." I clasped my hands together on the table and leaned forward. "I took the class, did my homework and made the offers. After all that, it doesn't seem I'm going to get the house."

"Oh — so that's how you're looking at things. Donna, I meet with people from all over the world and boy, do I hear excuses," George said, waving his hand to emphasize his point. "I failed at marriage, so why try again? I got fired from the last job, now I'm washed up. I want to expand my business, but I'll never get a loan so what's the use? And on and on they go. I tell my people those excuses signify a need to move into a more harmonious state of self-acceptance."

"Huh? What's that supposed to mean?" I asked.

> "It means we're all spiritual beings undergoing human experiences. You have to say to yourself and believe, 'Because I'm on this planet, I deserve to have a life of fulfillment on all levels.'"

"George, just because I say it, doesn't mean I deserve it. How do I know that?"

"Because, you're not on this planet to be poor, alone, or unhealthy." George shook his head and said, "I'm not saying those states of existence don't have purpose here. And there are great lessons of insight and wisdom to be learned from them, but, Donna, very few of us ask to be held in those states."

"That's what I mean, George. How do I get out of the state I'm in? I tried to stay positive, but after being rejected so many times, I'm beginning to believe I shouldn't have the house."

George raised his eyebrows. "Wait a minute. *You can't solve all your predicaments by covering up insecure feelings with positive thoughts.* That takes you only to survivor status — which is about where you are right now, Donna. Break new ground, find out what is limiting you. When you figure that out, you move beyond those barriers to a more wholesome belief system. That's a giant step toward your goal. *Don't hold yourself back. Let yourself be powerful. Get in there and fight for what you want.*" He grinned and threw up his hands. "I'm off my soap box now."

I shook my head dejectedly and said, "What's limiting me is that I don't believe that I deserve this house. You say otherwise. How can you be so sure I deserve this house?"

"You have to do the work first. Just how did you ask for the house?"

"George, I already told you all that."

"What I mean is, Donna, do you ask for it every night?"

I slumped back into my chair. "Every day — I ask for it every day."

"Do you ask if it's for your highest good?"

I thought it over and said, "I guess so. It's perfect — the layout — the view." It even has a suite over the garage for my office."

He grinned. "Here's the point — what you need to do when you ask for something:

> Get real clear, see it in your mind,
> say it out loud, and, finally, ask
> if it's for your highest good.
> You want it to serve you on all
> levels — emotionally, physically,
> spiritually and financially."

"That's what highest good does?"

George nodded. "This house will give you roots and make you work real hard. There's always plenty to do and fix when you own a house. Drive me on over there." He rose to his feet and smiled. "Whoever thought you'd be Susie Homemaker?"

In the car I said, "George, there's tenants in the house. They probably won't let us in."

"Don't let that stop you. We can pull the car in the driveway. Don't you want to own this house?"

"How about parking across the street?"

"I thought you wanted this house."

As we drove down the street, I noticed George staring off to one side of the road. "Stop the car," he said, and pointed his index finger. "That house over there — now that fits you."

"George, that's it! That's the house."

"Perfect. Pull over."

I parked the car near a snow bank.

He sat staring at the house, then sniffed with satisfaction. "Have you done everything possible to own this house?"

"Yes." I went down the list of all I had done.

"Do you see yourself in it every day?"

"Well I used to. Now I'm losing faith," I said slouching down behind the steering wheel.

George turned to me and asked, "Donna, you watch television?"

"Of course I do. What are you getting at now?"

"You watch any of those marathon races?"

"A few. What are we talking about this for?"

"Humor me. Tell me about them."

"Okay — you and your parables." I sighed and said, "Well, they start running and eventually the leaders come out of the pack and are way ahead of the rest."

"Do they all stay out in front?"

"No. Some get cramps and others lose their energy."

"Now we're getting somewhere. What about those behind in the pack? Let's talk about one of those runners who keeps pumping along real steady like and stays focused. Did you ever see one of them pull out of the pack, move out in front and win the race?"

I nodded. "I've seen that before."

"How do you suppose they did that?"

"I guess they prepared and trained and showed up. They didn't lose sight of their goal."

George suddenly smiled. "You got it. Winners never waiver in their belief in themselves and they never give up."

Renewed confidence was slowly taking root. "Okay, George, I'm getting the picture."

"That's better. When you go home, ask if this house is for your highest good and don't lose sight of your goal. Get hopping and make another offer. Now how about you taking me on a little tour? The mountains are all covered in snow and I want to see what this lake is all about."

I sat mindless as a vegetable staring out the window. George's words had me thinking about a story a friend had recently told me.

"Donna," George said, "We aren't going anywhere until you start the car up and get driving."

Startled, I said, "Sorry. When I was skiing with my friend Kirk at Squaw Valley, he told me a story. We were at the top of the mountain and I'd been dragging myself around because I was depressed about the house. Kirk asked me how long had I been trying to buy the house. When I told him six months, he proceeded to tell me his story."

"Well, don't keep me in suspense, Donna. I want to hear it."

I laughed and said, "Oh boy. Now I'm the one telling the story. Okay — here goes. It all started when Kirk's high school teacher said he would never graduate from college. The teacher basically told him he wasn't going to amount to much. Well, he proved her wrong. He learned his goal-setting skills, went on to college and graduated."

"Is that the end of the story?"

"No, no. There's more. Kirk decided he wanted a Porsche Carerra. After hearing how much the car cost, he was pretty discouraged, but he wanted to own a Porsche. So, he shared his vision with friends and they all said an expensive car like that would drive him to the poor house. But, he was determined. So, one day a friend gave him a picture of a Porsche Carerra and, what do they call it — oh yeah — superimposed Kirk's name on the license plate. He hung it up on the wall, and he looked at the picture every day. He worked extra time, sold stuff he didn't need anymore, played night janitor — whatever he could do to put money aside for the car."

"What happened next?" George asked.

"Well, after fourteen months of sweat, and penny pinching, Kirk decided to shop around and check with car dealers. It seemed he was not fated to find the car of his dreams. One day, he phoned a local dealer in Sacramento and described the car he wanted and the man said they had the exact car on the lot. Problem was, George, they wanted twenty nine thousand dollars for it.

"A few days later Kirk went to Sacramento. The salesman showed him a lot of cars, but none like the one he wanted. Finally, he told the salesman, he might as well go back home."

"Did he go back home empty handed?" George asked.

"No. Here comes the good part. The salesman said, 'Wait a minute. I almost forgot. A deal just fell through on a Porsche Carerra. It's all prepped on the back lot.'

"When Kirk saw the car, he stopped dead in his tracks. Because, right before his eyes, was the exact car pictured on his wall at home. He couldn't believe it. He laid his hands on the shiny blue roof, closed his eyes, and looked up at the sky. 'This is the one,' he said.

"He negotiated and the very next day, he drove off the lot with his dream car. A happy ending — right, George?"

He was silent for a moment before he said, "Real nice story. Kirk's message to you was, 'if you want to buy a house, keep the faith and be persistent."

I turned and smiled at him. "While I drive, you think about what you're going to buy me for a housewarming gift."

In mid-January, I made another offer. The weeks passed with no word from Joanne. I kept reminding myself of what George had said every night before I went to sleep. If the house was for my highest good, I would have it.

One morning while I was getting dressed for work, Joanne called. "Happy Valentine's Day," she said, "to the most persistent person I have ever met. Other than you, I've not had a single offer on my house. So, I'm accepting your last offer."

I was elated, speechless. And my mind was already working out ways to create the money I'd need for the payments. I didn't get flowers or candy that Valentine's Day, I got my highest good instead.

I dialed up George to tell him the good news.

"Well, hi, Partner," George said. "You getting enough snow up there?"

"You bet, George. This year, I'm really waiting for Spring." I paused.

"Something going on with you, Donna? Something we need to talk about?"

"Yes! I got a present, George. A big, big present." It warmed my insides to hear him chuckle. He'd been right all along and we both knew it.

"Patience and persistence. Pretty amazing, huh, Donna? When are you moving in?"

"Not until summer. I don't know how I can stand the wait. Of course, it'll take that long to figure out how I'm going to make the payments."

"I believe in you. You'll do it."

I laughed. "George, that's just what I needed to hear. Now start thinking about that housewarming gift."

✈ ✈ ✈

From February to July, I checked out garage sales and newspapers for bargains. I couldn't afford a moving van, so I lugged boxes, hoisted mattresses and carted bulky furniture. I didn't mind because I was just excited to move in.

I had decided to rent out my "would be office space" over the garage and use my formal dining room for a temporary office. I hung curtains and drapes throughout the house and bought warm comforters for the bedrooms. My new sofa was a perfect fit for the living room and the new wallpaper added a fresh decorative touch to the warm woods inside. The focal point was my cherished collection of framed photographs on the mantle presiding over the stone hearth. As a reminder of how far I had come and how much I'd grown, I placed a picture of the plane crash in the very center.

So exhausted from working in the house, sleeping was never a problem. The house and I had adjusted well to one another and I felt safe and happy, but when I wasn't traveling, I suffered bouts of loneliness. I decided I needed a pet for company — a little warm blooded companion to love. As a child I had big red fluffy chow dogs, birds and cats. Nowadays I traveled extensively and my preference was a cat. I had in my mind a cuddly fluffy cat. So, every night before I went to sleep, I asked: *How do I find the right cat for me?*

It took a few nights, but in the early hours of morning, between sleep and wakefulness, she came to me. She was definitely fluffy, and white, with captivating blue eyes. She had the gray markings of a Himalayan on her face and tail and I heard, "My name is Sheba. I'm waiting for you. Come and find me." I climbed out of bed and paced the house talking to myself. I kept saying, "Sheba, Sheba, Sheba." I laughed silently. Just the name, Sheba, sounded *spoiled.*

The next day I scoured the newspaper ads looking for Himalayan cats. At one house, the mother cat grouched at me and the kittens ran away. At another house, the kittens ignored me. The next ad I answered belonged to a tiny elderly lady. She was a breeder and said her name was Kitty. She also said she had a daughter named Donna. Strange, I thought. My mother's nickname was Kitty.

I drove an hour and a half to reach her home. I liked Kitty right away and her animals were wonderful. I had ten kittens to pick from and while sitting on the floor playing with them, I wondered how I would make such a difficult decision. After awhile the kittens became bored with me and went off on their own — all except one. The determined little kitten tried to crawl up my leg and kept falling off. I finally put it on my lap and was admiring how beautiful she was when she climbed across my lap and into my purse. She just sat staring at me with those big blue eyes. At that instant, I knew she was my cat. Sheba!

Kitty laughed and said, "You would. She's the pick of the litter and the most expensive. I talked Kitty into taking payments and my cute, high-priced cat had a new mom and a new home. We bonded instantly. Sheba became my shadow, following me everywhere and of course, my bed was her bed. Even in the garden, Sheba was right next to me digging in the dirt with her paws. So, from a very young age, she learned about water, since I had to bathe my little dirt ball frequently.

This period in my life was a wonderful time for me: speaking, traveling, stacking wood and preparing my house for the cold fall and winter months. Sheba had grown into a healthy, exquisite cat. One evening during the first snowfall of winter, I lit a roaring fire and she curled up beside me. I had my journal in my lap and I gazed out at the snow covered pine trees and reflected on the reasons behind my contentment. I had a career, a house and a cat. At last I'd carved out a life for myself.

JOURNAL
Action Creates Attraction

I have created peace within myself and I understand what it means to live in one's highest good. For when I live in truth, I have balance between body, mind and soul and fewer obstacles to confront.

Buying the house wasn't easy. After so many offers and Joanne's continual rejections, it didn't seem like I would ever own my own home. I was single, female with no established credit and I had no money for a down payment. Those were my fears. With George's help, I overcame them and that's what carried me through. I actually raised my level of expectation and affirmed I deserved the house. I visualized and was persistent. Doing that, made it easier for me to accomplish what I needed to do. By centering my inside with the outside, I had attracted the house to me.

I learned what centering really means. Catherina kept saying "Be. When you have done all your work, climbed all your mountains and have energized your body, then you Be."

Raimund was also right. He said to exist with nature, and I am with nature. It's calming for me to be surrounded by mountains, trees and water.

And dear George said,

> "The more powerful your vision, the more it demands of you."

For my highest good, I have attracted the house of my dreams, a career I love and a wonderful, affectionate cat. And Universe, I'd like to attract the man I'll marry and step-up my business.

Do it now!
Live your dreams!
Action creates attraction!

SECTION III

THE DESTINY

Trust Your Intuition

Thanksgiving weather in the mountains was as unpredictable as winning the lottery. On this chilly 'turkey day,' the temperature was in the low thirties and the wind off the lake blustery. As I drove through the quaint town of Tahoe City, the last vestiges of the aspen and maple leaves frolicked in my headlights. I had nowhere to go but home for Thanksgiving dinner, which would most likely be chicken and not the traditional turkey feast. I was lonely but happy because I'd just finished writing a little book called *30 Days to Success.* and had delivered it to the printer's lock-box for the first of what I hoped would be many runs. During these past months, my fulfillment came in the form of hard work. And now, when I needed a break, I was left without a dinner date.

I was feeling pretty low and thinking my situation couldn't get worse, that is, until a grinding thump from beneath my four-wheel drive warned me it could. The steering wheel stubbornly resisted my twists and turns, but I somehow maneuvered the car to the side of the road. As I sat helpless for a few minutes, wondering what to do, a kind soul pulled up in a Jeep and offered to call a tow truck for me. I thanked her and sat back to wait.

After the tow truck had arrived and the driver was hitching my car to the back, I noticed another car pull up behind us. A man got out of the car and I recognized him as the owner of a local business. I'd had brief conversations with him, but I didn't know him well.

He walked over to where I was shivering in my light jacket and said, "Looks like you have a problem. Can I help? Do you need a ride?"

It wasn't unusual for a local to offer assistance. When it snowed in the mountains and our cars broke down, we all needed to be rescued at some time or another. Snow was blowing hard and drifting at the side of the road. I smiled up at him, thinking I had never paid much attention to how tall and good looking he was. I glanced back at the tow truck driver struggling with the hitch and said, "You know, that sounds great to me. I live just a few miles up the road and I'm freezing."

"I'm going that way myself. No problem." He stuck out his hand. "By the way, my name is Matt."

I shook his hand. "Donna. Glad you came along."

During the small talk on the drive home, I asked, "Why aren't you with friends and family feasting on all the Thanksgiving goodies tonight?"

"Actually, I was invited, but didn't want to be the odd guest with no date. How about you? Matt asked."

I laughed and said, "Me too. I mean, I don't have a date either."

He hesitated, then said, "How about you and I having dinner sometime?"

"Sure," I said. "I'll give you my number." After he dropped me off and I went inside the house, I smiled when I recalled how his eyes showed more than a flicker of interest. The night wasn't a total disappointment. I had met someone nice — and attractive.

That night was the beginning of a fun loving relationship between Matt and me. We searched out wonderful restaurants and attended all the latest movies. Month after delightful month our packed schedule included snow-skiing, hiking, tennis, boating, and we even bodysurfed in Hawaii.

One perfect day, when Matt and I were lying on a Hawaiian beach watching the waves roll in and enjoying a wonderful ocean breeze, he said, "This is my kind of life. I want to stay here forever. I don't want to go back to work."

I poked him playfully and said, "Dream on. We've been in Hawaii ten days. I love it here too, but it's time. Tomorrow we leave to go back home." Matt pouted all that night. The next morning while we were boarding the plane, he complained again about not wanting to leave Hawaii. His capricious frame of mind bothered me, but I wrote it off as mere "end of vacation blues."

We enjoyed one another's company, played hard and laughed a lot. I was shocked at how fast a year went by, then two. It seemed to me we had so much in common and I felt my prayers had been answered — marriage must be on the horizon. However, when I mentioned the "commitment" word to Matt, he'd say, "Hey, we're having so much fun right now. You're such a great traveling companion, Donna, and a super skier. Aren't you having fun? Let's not spoil it."

One day at the park adjacent to the lake, I was watching the children playing. I gazed up at Matt's tan face and said, "I really want a family. Honey, that's so important to me."

He swivelled his head and uttered, "Wow! Did you see that?"

I glanced where he was looking and said, "What?"

"That boat that just barreled by. What a gorgeous piece of craftsmanship that was."

After dinner that night, I was paging through a magazine and held it up to display a picture of a beautiful baby girl. "Look at this," I exclaimed. "Isn't she adorable? I want one just like her."

"Yeah, yeah. Hey, hand me the TV Guide," Matt said. " There's this great action movie and I think it shows tonight."

It took several times more, but I eventually picked up the pattern. Whenever I would mention a family, Matt would immediately run off to another subject. I figured I should concentrate on getting married first and worry about the family later.

When the lease option on my house was up, I was thrilled. Because I never doubted our relationship would develop into marriage, I decided to put Matt on the Deed of Trust. Soon after that, he moved in and set up his office in the house. The non-committal pattern persisted. I would ask, "What about our relationship? When are we going to get married? How about a small, romantic wedding in Hawaii? How does that sound?"

He would deflect my questions with his own. "Should we eat in, or out? Let's go sailing. A new trail just opened up — we should hike it before it snows."

I assumed most people had this problem before committing. For me, marriage didn't have to happen right away. I just wanted the reassurance of an engagement ring. But, also, at the back of my mind was the ticking clock. I wanted a baby.

More months passed and Matt and I kept busy planning our "to do list." I loved motivational speaking with a passion. Yet, when I attempted to share my work experiences with him, he would turn cranky. He made no secret of hating his work.

I would say, "As much as I care about my work, it's sad you don't even talk about yours."

His response was, "Then you should work more because you like it. I don't want to work anymore. I just want to live in Hawaii."

I figured he would come around in time. How could he not? I was doing everything to make him happy. But in truth, our relationship was beginning to slide and I felt it was my responsibility, my juggling act, to hold us together. Finally, one evening as we sat in the dim light of a warm wood fire, I summoned up the courage to say, "Look, when are we going to get married?"

I waited for an answer as we both sat in a room silent, but for the flames popping in the hearth. Eventually, he said, "Donna, I just don't have the money right now. I can't buy you a nice ring and I know you really want a beautiful diamond. You've talked a lot about getting married, but in reality, I'm hard pressed for cash at the moment."

I could have danced on air. "Is that all that's stopping you?"

He nodded.

Before I went to sleep that night, I had myself convinced the only thing keeping Matt and me from being married was a diamond ring. A very solvable problem. But, in my heart, I denied the deepening sense of emptiness, and that our relationship was not growing. I was still needy and wanting more of him. Even when I was with him, I felt lonely.

Over the next few weeks, Matt became more withdrawn. I found myself spending more time with Sheba than with him. I took frequent long walks to think things through. I felt unattached, detached and unconnected and I constantly asked the question, "Am I going to marry this man?" The answer that came up in me was always "no." I kept walking and asking, hoping the answer would change. It never did. When I repeatedly told him how much I loved him, he would smile and nod and continue reading, or watching television.

Finally, to shut me up, Matt said he would marry me, but only if I had enough money. In my mind, I rationalized that was manageable. I would work harder and make more money to take care of us. I even hired a marketing director and when she promised to triple my business in one year, I was thrilled.

Jeanette's experience was impressive. With my business in such capable hands, it would leave me more time to spend with my future husband. When I asked for references, Jeanette apologized and said it was next to impossible to track them down because she was new to the area and the people she had previously worked for were no longer employed by the same companies. Though somewhat uncomfortable with her explanation, I hired her anyway.

The next week, I was in Los Angeles during a speaking engagement when I decided to solve the ring problem. I went to the Jewelry Mart and purchased a beautiful diamond and sapphire ring for myself. After I'd returned home and Matt and I were together, I held out my left hand with the ring and said, "Hey, Mr. Bridegroom, look at this. You couldn't afford a ring so I bought it. Now we can get married. I even bought a stunning white dress, perfect for a Hawaii wedding."

His response was, "I don't want to talk about it right now, Donna. " Then he turned and walked away.

I followed him into the living room. "Why? Is business bad?" I asked.

"Yes," he replied

I paused to digest what he'd said and dropped the subject, but I wasn't going to let him off easy. I intended to bring it up again the next weekend, but Matt told me he needed time to think and was going away for the weekend — alone. I swallowed back my disappointment. I would sacrifice even my pride. I cried from the time he left until he came home again.

After he returned, he resumed his distant attitude. I figured the reason was his wallet, which was decidedly empty. Desperate by now, I became even more obsessed on getting a proposal of marriage from him. I clung to him hating myself. "Talk to me," I begged. "Let's have dinner. What's at the movies? Please, talk to me," I heard distress creep into my voice and felt humiliated. I knew I was over compromising, but I told myself everyone in a relationship had to compromise. And I wanted a child.

When he went off alone again for two more weekends, I knew something was definitely wrong, but I had become a pro at denial. A denial that lasted until a certain afternoon when Matt was out skiing — alone again. Call it destiny, or whatever, the volume was left turned up on his voice mail machine and I overheard a message from a woman saying: *"I really miss you, Matt and I can hardly wait until I see you this weekend in Carmel. The weather will be perfect for a bike ride."*

My heart plunged, setting my mind on a whirl. I felt light-headed and sank down on the sofa unable to accept what I'd just heard. How could this be? I had arranged everything so perfectly. I played the message over and over until I had no choice but to believe Matt was involved with another woman. I wanted to scream and hit the wall. This was the man I would marry — the man I'd have children with — my man.

I heard his car come up the driveway and quickly decided what I would say. I took several deep breaths to compose myself. Then, I walked outside and said, "I really missed you today, honey. How was skiing without me?"

Matt was unloading his skis and his back was to me. "Actually, it was great."

His words turned me inside out. A sudden boldness surged through me and I said, "It's been awhile and I've been working hard. Let's you and I plan something special for this weekend."

He turned, then frowned. He was thinking up a response. After a brief smile, he said, "I've already decided to spend this weekend on the coast."

A hot ball of anger knotted inside my stomach and I struggled to keep from screaming at him. But, this was my production and I calmly had to see it through to the end. "Oh, that sounds wonderful. I really enjoy the coast," I said.

"Well — I only made arrangements for me," Matt said tensely. "You said you had to work."

"I've taken Friday, Saturday and Sunday off. Thank you, honey. I'm really excited." I could actually sense his fear that I might upset his cozy plan.

He hid a thick swallow in his throat and turned away. "I don't think I can get reservations this late and I don't want us to stay in some dump."

I pushed on. "Let's just go. We'll find something."

"I don't have any extra money, Donna. I can't afford some fancy hotel for the two of us."

The tension between us was supercharged. "I'll pay. It won't be the first time." I had decided to give Matt three tries to be honest with me. If he wasn't truthful by the third try, the relationship was over. His sour look said everything and I exploded. I shrieked out angry words I'd never forget, "I heard on your voicemail about your arrangements this weekend with another woman." His eyes widened for an instant, but he didn't utter a sound. "If you meet with her, our relationship is over," I yelled. He still said nothing. "Say something!"

Matt turned away from me and walked into the house.

By the next day, I had calmed down, but, the thought of his leaving to be with another woman had me feeling raw inside. I begged him not to go.

"I'm going," he said. He packed clothes into a suitcase and walked out the door. I grew hysterical, rolled into a little ball, screamed and cried. My wonderful visions of having a husband and a child had gone out the door with him.

I was furious at myself. I didn't listen to what my gut told me when I took all those walks: "It's going nowhere — he doesn't love you — he's never going to marry you." I had forced and manipulated our relationship, convincing myself I could make it work. I believed if a man would just love *me*, I'd achieve self-worth. All the lessons I'd learned from the men I had previously dated were rolled into one — Matt. He was the ultimate reprimand for not learning my lessons well.

The next three days were emotional bedlam. When Matt returned, he acted as if nothing had happened and resumed his lifestyle of choice. The next week-end, when he disappeared again, I didn't say a word. I was in such a diminished state, I didn't know what to do. However, when he came back, I summoned up the courage and asked if we could talk. Matt's response was to get off the sofa, go into the bedroom, lock the door and turn on the TV.

By now, the chilling dread that I had made a colossal mistake by putting him on the deed to my home had turned to a hellish reality. I had to demand that he leave.

The next morning, what I feared the most happened. When I asked Matt to pack his things and move out, he said in a cold voice, "I'm on the deed and I live here and I'm not moving."

I smouldered with anger, but somehow maintained my composure. In the days following, the stress was unbearable. We treated one another like strangers. I couldn't sleep, lost weight and my work was suffering. The anxiety was making me ill and I couldn't heal myself with the two of us living together in a hostile environment. In a candid moment I said, "I want you and your affair out of here, Matt. I can't live with you in the same house."

His response was, "My condo is rented and I can't kick the tenants out."

I made several more attempts to make him leave, but he ignored me. I finally consulted an attorney. After some heavy duty negotiating, my lawyer struck up a deal with Matt. I would have to pay a ridiculous amount of money to get him out of the house and off the deed. My attorney convinced me it was the only way.

He said, "This guy isn't nice, Donna. You'll spend years in court if you decide to fight him and you need to get on with your life. An even worse scenario — what if you had married this guy and he cheated on you?"

I took his advice and resigned myself to paying the money. A hard lesson learned.

After Matt moved out, I discovered the 'other woman' was much younger than I and he had moved her in with him. I'd see them in town together, holding hands. I felt assaulted by self-doubt and an overwhelming sense of uncertainty. Again, I had myself convinced I wasn't pretty enough, thin enough, tall enough, young enough or smart enough. And if that wasn't enough, I was also financially strapped. Making mortgage payments and paying Matt off left me with nothing.

I went numbly through each day. Every night I thanked God for Sheba, but always the dull throb of loneliness pulsated throughout the house. I was nearing the same emotional state I was in before the plane crash — hanging on to life by a flimsy thread. Late one night as I tossed and turned I'd pushed myself to a despair that surpassed exhaustion. Desperate for sleep, I stumbled into the shower, turned the water on full blast and curled up at the bottom of the shower like a creature burrowing in and hiding from the world. The harsh spray pelted my body, I beat the tile with my fists and screamed out my anger, pain and fear. I don't recall how long I remained in that state before I sensed a sudden cold draft. I looked up and was startled to see Sheba had popped open the shower door with her paw. I was astonished to see her gingerly step into the shower and wade through the water to reach me. I smiled through my tears, somehow fathoming this wringing wet cat, in her unique way, was bestowing her own brand of comfort. I heard, "Meow!" and knew that meant "let's get out of here — now!"

I picked up Sheba, got out of the shower and wrapped towels around us both. Then, I laughed uncontrollably until tears ran down my cheeks. At least I had one healthy relationship in my life. Sure, it was with a cat, but I had never experienced an empty, unwanted feeling around Sheba. Only unconditional love. I dried her off and looked into her beautiful blue eyes. Her little motor turned on and seemed to say, "Look, mom, I know you want a kid real bad, but if you do a good job raising your four legged kid, you'll get a two legged child."

The next morning, for the first time in days, I climbed the steps to my office. It was time for work and I had to build my business to get out of debt. I had at least done something right when I hired my marketing director, Jeanette. Her job was to call clients and book speeches for me, and right now I couldn't afford to let my business lag.

Still weaning myself from depression and trying to sort out my life, I needed someone to take over for awhile. She was dependable, great on the phone, knowledgeable, out-going and had loads of confidence. When I saw my empty calender filling up with speaking dates, I was ecstatic. A few years younger than I, Jeanette dressed well and her trademark was the huge tote bag she filled with snacks, lunch and what seemed her entire life.

I spent limited time in the office because I had difficulty concentrating, but my confidence was increasing by the day. I still had days when my energy was so low, I couldn't make finger shadows on the wall, days when I cried over nothing and feelings of inadequacy stormed through me. I discussed the situation with Jeanette and told her the Matt story. She was so understanding and it was good to have such a strong shoulder to cry on.

She said, "Good riddance to him. I never really cared for the guy."

I plodded along, each day bringing me closer to my old self again. It all started to backslide on one memorable day when I couldn't find the portable tape recorder I used for dictation. I had looked everywhere and asked Jeanette, "Have you seen my tape recorder?"

She smiled, shook her head and said, "No, I haven't. Don't worry. It will turn up. You've been under so much tension, you probably just misplaced it."

I nodded, feeling my insides shift. I couldn't be that forgetful — or could I? "You know, maybe you're right," I said. "I can't find my travel alarm either."

"You probably forgot them at the last hotel you stayed at. Why don't you give the hotel a call. Stress can play weird games with your memory, Donna."

"Humm. I suppose that's why I can't find my travel iron. Though it's kind of scary, Jeanette — to think I might be losing it."

"I'm sure it is." She gave me a sympathetic smile and said, "No man is worth all the anguish you're going through. You just get yourself better and let me worry about the business end of things."

Her words were assuring, and I felt she meant well, but not knowing what was going on in my own business made me uncomfortable. I had to assume my responsibilities again and today, I decided, seemed as good a time as any to do just that. It might be what I needed to boost my shaky morale. I said, "I'm ready to sit down with you and go over the financials and the reports. When can you make time?"

Jeanette's face assumed a look of dismay. "I'm sorry, Donna. You know how busy I've been on the phone. I haven't had the time to get all that together, but I'll have it for you soon. Don't worry. You just relax."

I said, "I am relaxing, Jeanette, but I need to review that information." I could tell I had upset her and felt guilty at pressuring her. "Look," I said in a more congenial tone, "why don't I get on the phone and personally call some of the clients you have lined up for me. I always make a point to talk with the contact person before I do a speech."

"Plenty of time for that, Donna. I'm just closing these two big contracts and I don't want to lose them. Smile when you look up at that wall and see the monthly calendars filling up. Things are great. It's a beautiful day. While I close these deals, you take a nice long walk."

I had an uneasy feeling that her excuses were merely masking her dishonesty. I grudgingly wound up taking a walk — and thinking more about Jeanette. The apprehensive lump in my gut wouldn't budge.

The next morning I was in the office bright and early. When I opened the petty cash bag to take money out for postage, I was astonished to find it empty. "Jeanette," I asked, "what happened to all the petty cash? I put a hundred dollars in here."

She shrugged and said, "Maybe you used it all up and just forgot."

I tried to remember, but that only got me flustered and disoriented. Seemed that happened often these days — too often. I pushed the subject from my mind and said, "Okay — okay. How about I call some of the clients you booked?"

"I have to finish up what's on my desk, Donna, and then I'll get the files together." Jeanette smiled and cocked her head in thought, "Didn't you say you had to work up some new material for your speech. Why don't you do that first? I'll just — make a few more calls."

Her answer merely spiraled the nagging suspicion that everything was going wrong. I pulled myself together and decided, though I was anxious to see proof of my bookings, what she had said made sense. I'd been putting off refining certain parts of my speech and doing it now made sense. When Jeanette finished making her calls we could review the bookings together.

I was well under way with my changes and it felt great until I overheard heard her say some things that weren't right. When she got off the phone I said, "Jeanette, you're misrepresenting me. I don't speak on Negotiation."

She raised her hands in a gesture of reassurance. "Oh — Donna — you can speak on anything. Once we get the contract, we'll work through it."

"No," I insisted, "I do not speak on that topic."

Pointing her index finger at me Jeanette said, "I'm the marketing director and I'll handle this. This is not your area. Isn't that why you hired me? To run the business while you go out and speak?" She took a deep breath and stared at me with a dry smile. "Each of us must do what we do best."

I was so taken aback, I walked out of the office to calm myself and think. Again, what Jeanette had said made sense, but I felt intimidated and just now, threatened. Perhaps scared was a better description because I'd begun to question if the problem was her or me.

The next week the spare stapler disappeared. I brushed it off as being mislaid. When I commented to Jeanette that I was missing one of my video tapes, she merely said, "It'll turn up." I mentioned that with the calender so booked, the phones were exceptionally quiet. She said she'd kept in constant touch with the clients and there was no need for them to call. Another puzzle to worry about.

On Friday, that same week, I was expecting a large check to come in from a speaking contract Jeanette had closed. She would earn a large commission. For the first time since I hired her, she didn't come to work. Her boyfriend phoned and said she was ill and could he come by to pick up her commission check. I agreed and later that afternoon, he picked up the check. On the following Monday, still no Jeanette — and no phone call. I decided to phone her at home. When a message came back announcing the phone was disconnected, a chill sharp as an icicle ran through me. I frantically called the other numbers she had given me. Dead ends. I sat at my desk fighting down the rising wash of panic with deep breaths. Slowly, the resignation — the grave enormity of my situation settled in. Jeanette was gone. My head was spinning and I hadn't a clue what state my business was in.

I spent the next few days sifting through the piles of records in Jeanette's desk. Nothing made sense. When I noticed conflicting dates, I began calling the clients. That's when I discovered the numbers were phony. At first I didn't want to believe it; then I panicked. That was just the beginning. The bookings shown on the calendar were nonexistent. Money was missing. She had handled my banking and none of my records balanced. And then came the day I encountered a sight that left me so shocked I was beyond speech. An investigation leading to a search of Jeanette's apartment had turned up over one hundred twenty items stolen from me. She had packed more in her tote bag than just snacks and lunch.

When it was all over, I had less than one hundred dollars in my checking account and no future income. I stood at my office window and stared out at the lake. Hot tears burned in my throat and welled in my eyes. I could lose my home — everything. I was in serious trouble and needed a miracle to survive.

I stayed in bed for two days, feeling drained of all power, sobbing until the tears ran out. Ten years after the plane crash I was asking the Universe questions day and night. Invalid pity-me questions like: Why was I betrayed by the two people I trusted? Why do I deserve this when I already went through a plane crash? Then I would whine: I don't want to start over, I don't have the energy, I don't have a career and I don't have a man. On and on I went.

Late on the second day, Sheba climbed up onto the bed and curled up on my chest. She lay there purring and before long I had calmed and stopped the junk messages I was feeding myself. When I looked into her eyes, I saw, "*Mom, I love you, and by the way, I'm the only one who loves you. So, you better start paying attention to me because you and I have to put things back together. I like my house and I like my yard and I'm not moving. You better figure out how to make the payments."*

The next morning I decided to see Mel, my accountant, and ask his advice. He listened to my story and looked at my books.

He said, "Donna, here are the hard facts. Unless you have a hundred percent increase in your business within the next three months, you'll not only lose your company, but you'll lose your house as well."

"A hundred percent — I can't do that," I wailed.

"Donna, you teach this stuff. Now is when you get to see if it really works. You can't blame the boyfriend and you can't blame the marketing director. They're long gone," he said. "You have to get to work — and now. You built your business from nothing once before and you can do it again."

I sighed. "You're right, Mel. I know you're right, but I'm tired. I just don't have anything left. I feel. . . "

"You feel what?" Mel asked gently.

I bowed my head and said, "I feel like everything my mother told me was right. She'd say, "You want to much. You'll never get a man. Speaker? Ha. Who's going to pay you to speak when you have nothing to say? Get a career you can make money at." I looked up. "That's what she would say. Maybe she was right because, Mel, I'm forty, no husband, no kids and about to lose everything"

I left Mel's office feeling even more depressed and decided right then to head straight for the airport across the street. I checked into the flights going to Denver and was delighted to discover the fare was lower than ever. I booked a flight for the following weekend. Then, I drove home and called George.

I heard, "Hi partner. Where have you been keeping yourself?"

I was silent for a moment before I admitted the sad truth. "George, the reason I haven't called is because I didn't want you to know what was going on with me."

He said, "That sounds pretty serious."

"George, I've been such a fool," I blurted out. "I've made terrible mistakes. I was on top of the world, got over-confident and lost it all. I don't think I can start all over again."

George sighed and said. "It's time for you and me to do some heavy talking."

"I'm flying in late Saturday afternoon. Can we go to dinner Saturday night? Please, I really need your help."

"My time is yours, partner. Meanwhile you take it easy. Don't do anything rash," he cautioned. "Go hug your cat. I have to go now. See you soon."

I couldn't remember much about the flight. When I landed at the Denver Airport, I called George and took a shuttle to his favorite Mexican restaurant. The sun was brilliant, but the chill of hopelessness clouded over anything warm. I spotted him sitting at a table beneath a brightly striped umbrella, puffing away on his pipe.

"Hi Partner."

He waved me over and I gave him an affectionate hug. My heart came to life hoping he could perform a miracle and wash away all the past disappointments and mistakes.

After we sat down, George waited for me to speak. I heaved a deep, ragged sigh and said, "I'm so ashamed. I've blown a big hole in my life again. I believed things would continually improve after the crash. And for awhile, they did. I worked hard and accomplished a lot. And then, after tasting success, I turned victim. I can't describe the feeling, George, but I don't think I have it in me to start over." Tears flooded my eyes. I blinked them back.

"Hold on, Donna. "You're not thinking about doing anything to harm yourself, are you?"

I shook my head. "No, George. Though I have to tell you, I'd like to move to Montana and be a hermit on a mountain top. I"m so disappointed. People I loved and trusted deceived me."

"So you want to run away." George sat puffing on his pipe then finally said, "Well, you can't spend the rest of your life on top of a mountain. Have you forgotten already what life is all about? It's about growth and about learning to pick yourself up when you fall down."

"I understand all that," I said. "What boggles my mind is how I messed up so badly after everything I've learned. I'm older and I thought I was wiser. This shouldn't be happening to me."

George looked me straight in the eye and said, "Wait a minute, partner. Let's talk about what you've done right. Have you built a career you like?"

"Yes. I love speaking."

"Do you have a comfortable home?"

I nodded.

George chuckled. "And let's not forget about your cat. You idolize that cat."

I grappled with what he'd said. Didn't he understand I could lose the house — the business — that I could hardly afford cat food? "George, that's all valid, but it doesn't change the fact that I'm dead broke."

"Oh — I see. Well, I remember when you used to call me and say, 'I'm going to Hawaii. I have enough for plane fare and barely anything left for food.' And I'd say, 'You'll get yourself a job and do just fine.' And you did. What about the times in Los Angeles when we would meet for breakfast and you'd say, 'I don't have enough money for rent.' "

"That happened more than I care to remember" I said, thinking back to those very lean days. "I usually bought plants and pictures on credit and canvassed all the office buildings door to door. By the end of the day I had enough money to pay for the merchandise and my rent." I folded my arms tightly in front of me. "But, I don't think you understand, George. This is different. It's going to take more than selling plants and pictures to get me out of debt now. I'm in serious trouble."

"The only thing that's different is your attitude," he said, "and a lack of faith that you can pick yourself up one more time."

"I'm sick of the attitude stuff," I grumbled. "Why did this happen to me anyway?"

George squinted and I saw something flicker far back in his eyes. I knew he was reaching inside for another supply of the practical knowledge he kept stored within himself. He finally asked, "What are your fears, Donna? What's blocking you? Because, when you understand your fears, you'll know why this has happened to you."

I shifted uneasily, fumbling for words, because I didn't really want to state my fears. At the same time, if George was to help me, I had to be honest. "I hate admitting this," I finally said. "I — I'm afraid no man will ever love me, or marry me. I want a family — a child. The man I believed would give me those things left me for a younger woman. I foolishly put him on the deed to the house and it cost me a fortune to buy him off. He stole my pride and punched holes in my confidence. He duped me, George."

> ## "Your fears control you until you confront them.

You let this man steal your power, Donna. You knowingly gave it to him. That's a massive lesson to learn."

I just shook my head. "What did I do wrong? Why did I have to learn such a painful lesson?"

George turned thoughtful eyes on me. "Every soul on the planet has painful lessons to learn. Lessons are a fact of life, like breathing. Your patterns controlled you. You grabbed onto a man, not because he was a wonderful person and treated you well, but because you were needy. You stayed in that relationship because you were afraid to leave and thought there would be nothing better for you. You almost settled for an unhappy life."

"It sounds like my life today," I complained. "So — all right. Here they are — my fears — no man, no money and no child. How do I fix this, George? Stand on a corner and flag a man down like when I sold pots and pans?"

He chuckled. "This last man was the last of the worst of the men in your life. He was the essence of all the men in your past who have disappointed you. Now is when you can beat this pattern and never repeat it." He reached into his pocket and held out a pen. "Turn over your napkin. Take the pen and write his name on the left side and yours on the right." Reluctantly, I did as he asked. "Now, write down your three most important values."

I sagged back in my chair. George was relentless, but I wrote them down. "Love, family and work," I said.

"Okay. Write down what you believe his values are."

I didn't have to write. I would never forget them. "Freedom, fun and sex. Not one matches mine," I said.

George chuckled. "Do we have anything in common here? Of course not, because when your values don't match, you're in conflict. Give me the truth. If this same man came back to you and asked you to marry him, would you say 'yes'?"

He'd asked the question I'd been afraid to ask myself. The humiliating question I kept pushing to the back of my mind. Would I? Was I that desperate? I sighed and said, "I honestly thought I loved him, and yet it wasn't a loving relationship. Now that I'm away from it, I know we really didn't love each other. We filled each other's needs, but weren't growing as individuals.

I looked up at George and said, "No, I wouldn't want to marry him. He doesn't want love and commitment, doesn't want a family and he hates his work."

George said with a grave nod, "How long have you known that? At what moment did your intuition tell you he wasn't the right man for you?"

My mind flipped back to when Matt came into my life. "About a year after we met. When the fun stuff wore thin. I knew he really didn't love me because he told me he didn't want to get married. I was so sure I could change his mind and I kept asking and he kept avoiding. George, I was so needy, I didn't see the big picture."

"There you go. Now, that's real honesty. You have to first love yourself to attract the right man who will love you.

> ## You can't manipulate love and you can't force it. It has to flow naturally."

"But, George, didn't the plane crash teach me to love my-self?"

"You thought you did, but you weren't totally committed. You have to believe it with every cell in your body. We may have the knowledge to understand, but when we're obliged to apply our-selves in a real life situation, that's where we we're tested." He paused. "You tell me you don't want to marry this man. Then, what do you want?"

I sat with my head inclined thinking and there it was again. The one thing I really wanted. I gazed up at George and said, "I figured, by now, I'd be married and have a child. I just don't understand why that hasn't happened yet. I see couples everywhere and here I am — still single. I'm beginning to wonder if the traditional path is right for me."

George nodded. "You have a different destiny — lessons to learn. Each man in your life gave you an opportunity to learn another lesson. From some you learned patience, others — the skill of communication, several more — the pain of betrayal and lies. Today, you understand it's common values that support a relationship, not just common interest — and that relationships can't be forced. The marriage — the relationship — has to be what both people want.

> Trust your intuition and you
> receive the gift of knowing.

The choice is always yours to learn from your experiences. A lesson you learned well is financial independence. Donna, you will get out of debt and become richer from the experience."

"George, you really are my saint. You have such vision — such faith in me."

> "All things are possible
> if you believe.

Say, I'm hungry," he said and reached for a menu. "Can we order dinner now?"

I laughed. "Oh, sure. But, I don't know about the eating part. I have tons more to tell you."

While we waited for our food, I gave George a full accounting of what happened with my marketing director. Then, as we ate, I hammered out more questions. "How could she steal from me when I trusted her so?"

George swallowed a fork full of tamale and said, "She sensed your fear, Donna, and she knew you were in a weak state. You hadn't regained your power. You were afraid you weren't smart enough to run your company and she picked up on that."

I just looked away.

"I know what you're thinking, Donna — that you could have done without the experience. But, the lesson was attracted to you so you could learn from it. Good you got two of your greatest fears out of the way at the same time."

"You think that's good," I said. "I think it's bad."

George said. "Accept you're smart enough to run your business and do it."

I rolled my eyes. What was left of it.

"When you went to college in Hawaii, and you didn't have enough money, were you afraid to sell pots and pans?"

"Yes. I had fears and no confidence. I even got fired. But, Chuck gave me another chance and I became a very good sales person."

"Yup. And when it looked like you were going to die in the plane and the flames were all around you, you faced a tremendous fear when you walked through the flames to save yourself. You conquered your fears, Donna. You did it then and you can do it again.

> **Stop looking at problems as problems. Make them learning lessons."**

"George I — I was afraid I'd be alone without a man, or a child to love me and I compromised myself. It's over and I'm never, not ever, going to repeat that lesson again."

George laid down his fork. "Boy, have I been waiting years to hear that. You're finally claiming your own power — and doing what's best for your highest good."

I smiled. "I'm a slow learner, but I'm finally getting it."

"By the way," he said, "speaking of your highest good, let's talk about the marketing director. Did I hear you say if she had job references?"

"I asked for them, but she always had excuses."

"Did you ever see those weekly reports you talked about?"

I sighed and said, "She was always running behind."

Then, George asked, "Did you ever call any of the clients she had booked?"

I shook my head, slumped my shoulders. "I should have known, George, because I had that feeling in my gut that something was wrong. I was upset over the man issue and didn't pay attention. She made it so easy and I just — let her take over."

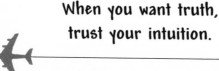

**When you want truth,
trust your intuition.**

"There were times when she said certain things I thought weren't right. When items turned up missing from my house and my office, I couldn't put my finger on it, so I just blamed myself."

"You intuition gave you the answers, but you weren't paying attention," George said.

> There are no accidents. Everything happens for a reason. Once you understand your learning lessons, you'll achieve inner wisdom.

I got very quiet. His words had stirred up strong feelings of inner awareness. I sensed a message was coming through to me. A message I couldn't ignore. The next question just popped out. "George, how long have you been looking after me? I don't mean back when I first met you in Hawaii. I mean — even before then."

He got quiet, then asked, "Did that question come from you?"

"Well, yes, but I didn't have to think to ask it. It just sort of — materialized."

"In that case, it's time for you to know," George said, and again the clear light appeared in his eyes. "Call it what you want to call it, every person on the earth has someone looking after them. Some people need a little extra help, like you. When you were six years old and in the hospital with malnutrition, that's when the assignment to watch over you came to me. From then on, I kept checking in on you. There's all kinds of ways to do that. You might say I've done my homework." He chuckled. "And then some."

I hadn't realized my mouth was hanging open until I closed it. "You mean like ESP?"

"Kind of, but far beyond the normal range," George said.

"I was there when you had heart surgery at sixteen and that clot almost took you away."

I sat in a stupor. "You were — there?"

"Yup, sure was. There's telepathy, even clairvoyance that can give you the information you need. Donna, you know when you know. Everyone has the gift. You just have to develop it." George got very quiet, then said, "I've been assigned twelve people to look after. Sure, I help a lot more people than that, but twelve people need my personal guidance." He laughed. "I have to say you're more trouble than all the other eleven put together. None of the others have your energy, or your questions. You're a pistol."

I swallowed hard and said, "Are you saying you've been with me since I was six years old? You looked after me? You were sent by a power greater than both of us? That you — accepted and loved me? George, that means, no matter how much I messed up all those years, you still loved me?" I stared down at my plate. "I don't know what to say."

George smiled.

> "Life is pretty simple. It's man that complicates it. Just love yourself and love others."

He grinned and said, "Are you actually speechless? First time I've ever seen that."

The waiter came to remove our plates and George said, I'll have a cup of high octane coffee and the young lady — give her the unleaded kind." When the waiter had left, he said, "Caffeine right now will put you right over the top."

I smiled. "I guess it boils down to my believing I was betrayed by people I trusted and loved when I should have been strong enough to trust myself."

"You got it, Donna. Your maker never gives you more than you can handle. Your problems don't look so bad when you put them in a pile with everyone else's.

> **When you have a choice to either pick out someone else's problem, or take back your own, we humans take back our own, because our problems don't look as bad as the other guy's."**

George became more serious than ever. "Donna, you've done a real good job listening today. Now, I want to tell you something and you listen real close. I'll always be with you — always. The soul goes on. All you have to do to connect with me is get real clear and quiet, say my name and think about me. You'll feel an awareness that I'm with you. Trust it."

"George, you're so serious. I just don't think I have that gift."

"Didn't you have visions and a feeling about the plane crash before it happened?"

I nodded. "But, I didn't listen to them."

George ignored what I said, took a minute to light his pipe and went on talking. "And a vision about your cat, Sheba? Exactly what she would look like? That she was coming to you? Didn't you trust that?"

I hesitated. "Yes."

"You have the gift," George said in a tone I had never heard him use before. "You just don't know it yet."

I recalled my vision and remembered I still had to ask him one important question — the one I desperately needed the answer to. In a way, I was almost afraid to ask because the answer might not be the one I wanted. I took a deep breath and said, "I had a vision about a baby girl. George, am I ever going to get her?"

For a few seconds his eyes followed the smoke from his pipe as it spiraled into the air. Then, he looked straight at me and said,

"You will have a daughter. She'll come to you. Count on it. She's a pistol, just like you. She loves life and has your energy. You'll have your hands full. She's a leader and has a mind of her own."

His words warmed me with a happiness I hadn't felt in days. "You sound so sure, George. Is she going to be right for me?"

"Oh yes, and you'll know. Stop the worrying. No matter what, I promise I'll be there when you get your daughter." He stood up and stretched his arms "Now, enough of this serious talk. Just remember, I'll be there. Let's you and I go for a walk."

George seemed to know right where he was headed. I followed him to a path that took us behind the restaurant. A delightful stream trickled on one side of the path. On the opposite side, beautiful mansions with perfectly manicured yards backed up to a forest of lush green trees.

We strolled in silence, as we often did, while George smoked his pipe. After a while he said, "Donna, "don't ever give up on your dreams. Remember what I said about so many people living in pain and disappointment. You can help them because you now understand it," George said, moving slightly ahead of me. Then, he stopped so suddenly I almost ran into him. I saw two rabbits on the path, as motionless as a still-life picture. Then I noticed even the birds had hushed their chirping. The rabbits were staring at George, but they didn't seem afraid. Three small sparrows stayed very close to George and didn't fly away. There seemed to be a communication between him and the creatures. After awhile, George nodded his head. The rabbits hopped away and the birds flew into the trees, chirping again.

I turned to him and said, "Wow! I've never seen you do anything like that before."

He chuckled. "I was just having a little after dinner conversation with my pals."

"But there was no sound," I said.

"Donna, I just gave you a little illustration of what we were talking about earlier. If you want to put a name to it, it's a form of telecommunication. I send out a message — the birds and animals receive it. They send out a thought and I get it."

"Most people make noise when they talk to the birds and animals, George. They don't do what you just did," I pointed out.

"Because they believe they can't," George said. "Animals talk to us all the time. We just don't listen. I was just telling them how much I love them and we were conversing about nature. People communicate the same way with each other — transmit messages back and forth. Your higher consciousness deciphers the message. Don't you communicate with Sheba?" he asked.

"Yes, but I have — you know — a little dialogue."

He shrugged. "How about when the phone rings? Don't you sometimes have a strong sense of whose calling? Well, all I do is skip the words and send it out. If I stood here talking to the animals, people would think I was nuts."

"You know, now that you mention it George. . . once when I was sick with a fever and had to do a speech the next morning, Sheba climbed up on my chest and stayed there until my fever broke. She actually helped me get better." I thought for a moment and said, "But Sheba and I understand each other."

"All living creatures are connected. The telepathy is right inside you, Donna, but you have to work at it."

> **Keep meditating and when you do, get quiet enough to stop the inside chatter.**

"You know what I mean," he said. "Don't worry about paying the phone bill while you meditate. And when you get visions, believe in them. It's your higher self communicating the truth."

"I'm glad I came to Denver," I said. "You've given me so much to think about, George. You've shared with me more than you ever have. And yes, I'm sick and tired of being sick and tired. I'm done forcing things to happen because it doesn't work. I want the situation to flow naturally."

We turned to go back and George said, "Like I keep telling you, Donna, life is simple. Remember your values and stay connected to the man upstairs. We only have so much time on the planet. Use it wisely.

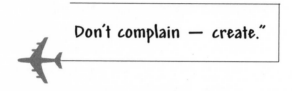

> Don't complain — create."

I said, "I honestly want to raise my life to a higher level. It's just that starting over is so hard."

"Sure it is. I've dealt with some contractors and you know what they say? *"If you're going to build a skyscraper you have to go deep down to build a strong foundation."*

"Do I have to go this far down, George?"

He chuckled. "That depends on how high you want to go."

"I get the message," I replied, feeling calmer than I had in weeks. "Everything is making sense now. I can see so clearly how I botched up my belief system. George, I'm very grateful. Every time I've needed your help, you've given me your time, your wisdom and your love. I don't know how to thank you for all that you've done for me."

George said, "This is how it works. I again saw the same burning light in his eyes. "When someone comes to you and needs help, give them a guiding hand."

"How will I know how to help them?"

"Like I always say, *'You'll know when you know'*. The teacher can't always be with the student. I can't always be with you. Situations crop up when you alone will have to recognize the truth. When you ask for truth, you'll get a clear answer. Believe what it tells you. Everyone on this planet has opportunities to develop their conscious awareness, or as I say, a knowing. I want you to work real hard to develop this level of your consciousness. Donna, you have feelings all the time. When you do, pay attention to what they're saying and trust them. It could be what some call a sixth sense, or keen intuition — or perhaps a fleeting moment that carries a strong message. Maybe it's a persistent little that voice keeps telling you something and you feel it deep down inside. Moments of clarity can help speed up a positive action, or warn you when an action isn't right for you. Just don't doubt when it comes to you.

> **Believe and act on what your knowing tells you."**

It seemed as if George was cramming me for a final exam. He had a sense of urgency about him, like I had to understand everything he was saying to me. Whatever his reason, I would do my best to listen and learn from him. Perhaps it was that my hard-to-learn lessons had precipitated a turning point for me and we both sensed it. I turned to him and said, "George, I'm not always sure what my knowing is."

"The problem is not unique to the human race, Donna. You, like everyone, have the gift of inner awareness. That means what rings true inside of you is the truth. The more you develop and trust it, the more you'll use it. It can come to you in several ways:

a vision, a message, a sense — or just a feeling. Everyone experiences all these things at one time or another. Not everyone pays attention."

We were walking so slow we had almost stopped. I took note of George's exceptional patience and how intent he was to make his point.

"Now, getting back to when people come to you, tell you their life is not good and ask for help. Maybe you can talk to them about meditation, or take a nature walk, or suggest a book. Or just be a good listener over a cup of coffee. Everyone runs into walls from time to time, but they have to want to break them down. Donna, look back at all those times when you met me at the crack of dawn for breakfast. You were serious and committed to learn. Once you've done your best to help and people ask, 'How do I thank you?', tell them to pass on a helping hand to someone else."

George and I walked all the way back to my hotel. "I'll meet you at your hotel coffee shop at six for breakfast," he said, "then I'll drive you to the airport."

Just as he turned to leave the lobby through the revolving doors, I remembered I had forgotten to tell him about my little book. "Wait, George, wait a minute," I called out and ran to catch up with him. "I want you to read something."

He chuckled. "Sounds important."

"It is and I need your opinion." I handed him a copy of my *30 Days to Success* book. "I just had five hundred of these printed up. It's my contribution to the literary world."

George took the book from me and perused the title thoughtfully. "Is that all it takes? Thirty days?"

I laughed and said, "I've been working on it thirty years, but I didn't have this book to start me off. It's a realistic jump start plan with strategies and self-talk — a little book with big information to get you what you want."

"It doesn't matter — thirty years, thirty days, thirty hours or thirty seconds," he said. "What matters is that you get it. I'll look it over tonight. I've got a good feeling about it."

True to his word George arrived at the coffee shop early the next morning. This time, we both ate a pancake breakfast, and afterwards George drove me to the airport. As we walked to the gate, he reached into his pocket and handed me back my *30 Days to Success* book. "This is going to be a winner for you. It's good stuff," he said, "and it'll help a lot of people. Now, when you get home, be sure to put this copy in a safe place."

When the call came to board my flight, I gave George a hug and said, "This was a tough learning lesson about not being needy. Thank you." I grinned. "Hey, this plane isn't going to crash is it?"

He chuckled, "No way, Donna. You can't get off the planet that easy. Now get happy."

I walked toward the boarding ramp, then turned to wave.

I heard, "Get happy."

JOURNAL
Trust Your Intuition

It was great to see George. My energy, my spirits had hit rock bottom before we talked. A few hours with him calmed me down and got me centered again. And he was right. I did need to make my value list and now I needed to stick to it. I thought long and hard on the plane ride back home. I feel I'm connected to planes because fate has me doing my best thinking flying in the air. And intuition does play a big role in my thinking. When I listened to my intuition, I made more confident choices. When I didn't listen to that wise gut feeling, I became a victim.

My commitment is to release denial, to trust my intuitive feelings, whether a vision, a message, or an intuitive sense. I'll ask more questions, search out the answers and believe I'll invite truth that's natural and not forced. Just as George has said,

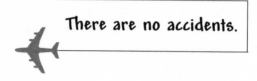

There are no accidents.

I'll maintain the faith that my daughter will come to me. I'm past forty and my original plans for having children didn't work. So now, I'll check out adoption agencies and find those that will consider a single mom who is no spring chicken. And I'll rebuild my business bigger than ever. The motivation to keep me focused is knowing my daughter is coming. And I have a wise man's stamp of approval to guarantee that.

This was a tough lesson, Universe, and I claim it. My neediness was a major part of the problem. I accept this lesson and vow to never repeat it. I resolve to live in my values, trust my intuition and believe in my visions. Intuition is like tuning in my car radio, ridding the static and listening to clear communication. The answers that create the knowing lie inside me.

> **I'll trust my intuition to guide me to the knowing revealed in my visions, my messages and my intuitive sense. 'You know when you know.'**

Center Your Energy

I centered all my energy into work and pushed forward — day by day. It was a rare week when I worked only six days. My basic diet was rice and water and water and rice, but I was fighting my way out of debt.

Only a few months after visiting George in Denver I landed a large contract for a bank in Southern California. It saved me from near bankruptcy. I had put my teaching degree to good use by conducting a seminar called "Is Your Attitude Showing?" I knew the material well, but I had to laugh at the irony of the situation. Still in the process of adjusting my own attitude, here I was teaching it to others. But I knew it didn't happen by mere accident. Teaching 'attitude' guaranteed I would learn it.

I frequently called George for a dose of his philosophical optimism. He'd say something like, *"Be happy — love today and yourself and love the opportunity to work."* I heard the pride in his voice when I told him I was cleaning up my debts.

He said, "A big round of applause to you, Donna. I never doubted you would succeed."

I was still making payments to the ex-boyfriend and I kept pestering my accountant Mel with the same question: "Do I have enough money to go out for dinner yet?"

He'd grin and shake his head. "Nope. Keep cooking that rice and water a while longer."

My spirits soared when a host of new opportunities opened up for me. I had my own TV show and I'd landed international accounts in Canada, New Zealand, Australia, England, Finland and the Caribbean. I frequently phoned George to share my travel adventures with him. He laughed when I said, "George, I'm amazed to find that people are the same the world over."

"I've been telling you that for years," he replied.

During one of our more memorable conversations I asked, "When is my daughter coming?"

George was silent for a moment and then he replied, "The time is getting close, Donna. Just be patient a while longer." And when you get her, remember, I'll be there. Now, be happy and get to work."

The months of promise turned into years of anxiety. I'd made nine attempts to adopt and though I was praying as hard as I could, it hadn't happened. The ex-boyfriend was finally paid off, my career was doing well and I had positioned myself to support a child. Everything in my life had turned around for the better, except for the waiting.

Early one evening in October, I had just returned from a trip and the telephone rang. It was a woman from Denver named Jeannie — one of twelve people George had worked with. He had introduced me to her once when I had a long delay in Denver. He'd confided that ten men and two women were assigned to him for spiritual guidance and mentoring.

She said, "Donna, I have news for you. George crossed over today. He's with the man upstairs."

The shocking news left me trembling with an ice cold lump in my heart. "Oh, no," I gasped. "I talked to him just before I left on this last trip." I kept turning Jeannie's words over in my mind. Crossed over — George. The words clogged in my throat. "I can't believe it. . . How. . .?"

"It was very sudden," Jeannie said. "He became ill in Texas and was diagnosed with cancer. The doctor admitted him into the hospital right away. George was gone within a week."

I opened my mouth to speak, but her news had shocked away all but a few words. "Thanks for calling me," I whispered. I hung up the phone and paced the room, swallowing back tears of indescribable sorrow. George would say I was wearing a hole in the carpet because I walked in circles. I kept calling his name and repeating, "It can't be. It just can't be. You said you would always be here for me. I can't believe it. Why didn't you call me when you knew? Why didn't you call me, George?"

I eventually quit my pacing and sat down on the sofa. I closed my eyes and concentrated on what he looked like, the scent of his cherry pipe tobacco, his voice. "Talk to me, George. I feel so alone — so sad. Give me a sign." I pleaded — I meditated — nothing. And then I prayed until my grief filled the room. Still nothing. Perhaps George wasn't where he was meant to be yet, I rationalized. It takes time to make the journey to the other side. I should wait awhile and try again.

I badly needed a cup of tea to calm me down and headed for the kitchen. Half way there, I stopped dead when a flash, like a current of communication, passed through me.

> "You can't contact me the traditional ways, but even if you can't see me, Donna, I am with you in spirit. I'm your guide."

I gasped as a wave of happiness surged though me. I was granted the acknowledgment that George was still with me. My prayers and meditation had reached him and he had transmitted his answer to me. I smiled as I ran water in the tea kettle. I knew as sure as the heart grieves, he would contact me again.

I had worked straight through the holiday season, without a break. I felt empty and lonelier than I could ever remember. I found myself several times reaching for the phone to call George, then a rush of sadness when I remembered he was no longer on the planet. Though I often tried, it became more difficult to re-call George's face to mind, or even the way he held his pipe, but I never forgot the expression in his clear, penetrating eyes. I hadn't given up on hearing from him again. During my medita-tions I regularly asked for signs that he was with me. On one occasion after my meditation, I lit my favorite scented candle and asked that he contact me. After I waited several minutes and nothing happened, I asked again. "George, please I need a mes-sage from you — anything. I don't remember how much time had passed before I saw an image begin to take shape. I couldn't make it out at first, but it became clearer, and I recognized the face of an infant baby girl with dark hair, wrapped in a pink blan-ket. I heard, "Mommy, I'm coming to you." She faded away and a message appeared: *"Between May twentieth and July fifth this year, and my name is Mariah."* The communication was clear and undeniable. I *knew* my child would come to me soon.

George and I had talked about my wanting a child so often, I knew his presence had attracted the vision and the message. A baby girl named Mariah was coming to me. She had dark hair and would arrive between May twentieth and July fifth, some six months from now. I smiled recalling the conversation George and I had years before.

He said, "We all have the gift of vision and insight, but only a few of us take the time to develop our *knowing*. Your visions match your personality, Donna. You're quick, dramatic and a decision maker. Likewise, your visions emerge quickly and they're compelling and certain. It's different for everyone — some fast, some slow. What matters is when you do get those glimpses, don't discount them."

I didn't believe for a moment my vision was fantasy. As I leaned back against the sofa another of George's blooming parables came to mind. I could heard him talking as though he was standing right next to me:

> *Two childless couples went to a wise man and asked him to grant them children. Well, a year later, the couples returned. But, only one couple had a youngster. The wise man asked each couple what took place after their first visit. The couple with the youngster said, "We went out and bought a baby carriage and waited for our child to arrive." The second couple shook their heads real sad like and said, "We didn't do anything."*

The next day I went shopping. I bought a crib, a rocking chair and a bunch of stuffed animals. Then, I came up with an idea to decorate Mariah's room in an animal theme. When I told my friends my daughter was on her way, some looked at me strangely and offered a blank smile. Others explained as gently as possible that maybe I was a little old to raise an infant and not to be disappointed if the adoption didn't happen. Some even said my cat would resent Mariah. I told them all the same thing, "I will never give up my dream. My daughter is coming." I did a little more research on what a new baby needed and made out my baby shower list.

I registered with another adoption agency run by a single mother and sympathetic to single women. Then came the real test of faith. The woman asked me to write a check for the full cost of the adoption before I even had the child. I immediately got on the phone and landed two corporate speaking engagements. I was overjoyed when the deposits came in. Besides the money, the agency wanted an immense amount of information about me. I gave them all the information I could and clung to my belief that Mariah was coming.

In Spring, I received a call from the agency. An expectant couple from Reno, Nevada had selected me as a prospective parent for their baby. I met with them and thought they were great people. A few days later, a sonogram disclosed the baby was a boy. Though excited to be chosen, I still believed the right child for me was the baby girl I had envisioned. The agency sensed my hesitancy and cautioned me I might not have another opportunity because I was an older, single applicant. They said they didn't know when, or if, there would be another opportunity like this.

That night I prayed for guidance, asking if I was the right mother for this boy. "What is his destiny?" I asked. I sensed he'd be a quiet child, computer aware and technically focused. I realized I couldn't fill his needs. I called the birth parents the next day and learned they had another couple in mind besides me. "What are they like?" I asked.

"Rather quiet and they run a computer business from their home. Nice," they said.

Perfect parents for the boy, I thought. I paused to think over how I'd explain why I couldn't adopt their child. I said, "I'm very honored I was the first choice to raise your child, but I'm not the right person to help fulfill your son's destiny. He belongs with the couple."

The agency was livid. I was clearer than ever. I knew deep down inside, my daughter was on her way.

Nine days later, the agency called again. The woman said, "Donna, expectant birth parents from Las Vegas have selected you to be the adoptive mother for their baby girl. She's due to arrive in six weeks, at the end of June. I can't believe someone chose you again so soon after you turned down a child. It just doesn't happen," she added.

In a rush of happiness, I said,

"You know when you know.

Would you believe at the beginning of this year, I had a vision? I knew beyond a doubt my daughter would arrive between May twentieth and July fifth." Tears welled up and I took some deep breaths. "You see, a dear friend of mine told me to always trust my knowing."

I was given permission to contact the birth parents. I rehearsed what I would say, picked up the phone, put it down, made a sandwich, took two bites and rehearsed what I would say again — with my cat. I tried dialing the phone two more times before I made the actual call.

The conversation was strained at first. I learned the mother was named Kel, and Connor was the father. We were all nervous and I kept running off at the mouth to fill in space. After awhile, when we became more comfortable, the conversation got under-way. I had so many questions, but didn't want to ask them all during our first chat. I learned Kel was divorced and the mother of a son before she met Connor. Kel and Connor eventually had a daughter together who is now three years old. And Connor is also the father of their forthcoming child. The problem was they had since split up and he was seeing another woman. Kel couldn't possibly support another child on her own and Connor wasn't working. Under the circumstances, they both agreed it was best to put their expected baby up for adoption. Kel thought my quali-fications were very impressive, but what impressed them most was the questionnaire and bio I had completed for the agency. Though single, my education, attitude and stability had convinced them I could provide a loving environment for their child. Over all, the conversation left me feeling extremely optimistic.

Before we hung up, I agreed to fly Kel and Connor into San Francisco to meet with the agency. After that, I would drive them to my home in Lake Tahoe, take them to dinner and fly them back to Las Vegas the next day. They both liked the idea and consented to bring their daughter, Mandy, with them. Kel's son, they said, was away visiting his grandparents for two weeks.

On the day they were due to arrive, I waited at the airport gate searching for a pregnant Kel. I wondered if I should hug them, shake hands, or just wave. When the departing passengers had thinned out to mere stragglers and I'd just about given up hope, the three of them came up the ramp. Kel explained she was so nervous, they were the last to leave. I bent down and gave little Mandy a hug and the tension was broken.

I liked the birth parents instantly. They were in their mid-twenties and wholesome, but it was easy to see they were not sophisticated in a worldly sense. Kel looked like a typical expect-ant mother — tired, but radiant. Tall and blue eyed, she wore her lustrous brown hair pulled back in a pony tail. Connor, also tall, had a slim build and thick dark hair cast with red. He carried their only suitcase. I checked my watch and said, "We better get a move on. We have just enough time to make it to the agency."

The meetings with the agency were conducted individually and behind doors. There was droves of paperwork to explain to Kel and Connor and it allowed time for Mandy and me to get to know each other. She was a sweet, outgoing child. As the minutes dragged on, the tension of the situation had formed cold little lumps of fear in my stomach. By the time I met with the woman from the agency, I had non-stop questions: Do they like me? What did the medical records say? Is the child healthy? Can they change their mind at the last minute? In a noncommittal tone, she said everything looked good.

During the drive to Lake Tahoe, I learned we all had the same English-Irish background and that we shared some common interests: books, movies, a love for the outdoors — qualities I hoped would be endowed on the child.

Kel and Connor were instantly attracted to Tahoe. They admired my home and raved about the animal decor in Mariah's room. I felt doubly optimistic when Kel kicked back in the rocker with a sigh and said, "I could stay here forever." Connor, on the other hand, was impressed by the pine trees, the lake and how majestic the mountains were. When he asked questions about my educational background and checked out the books on the shelves, I eagerly provided the answers. He even asked what college subjects I had excelled in. He sheepishly admitted always wanting to go to college, but his parents didn't have the money and he had no guidance. I found myself enjoying our conversations about my speaking, the places I had traveled to and even exchanging different opinions. Kel remained the listener. I sensed she felt timid about contributing to the conversation.

After dinner, Kel put her energetic daughter to bed and said good-night. I sat propped up in bed with the light on, thinking about the events of the day. I couldn't focus on my book and was too wound up to sleep. It was heartwarming to learn the birth parents were more accommodating than I expected and I felt so comfortable around them. And little Mandy was thrilled when I gave her a fluffy stuffed rabbit, identical to one of Mariah's. Too bad they weren't a couple any longer. Kel's warm, down-to-earth quality was an interesting contrast to Connor's underlying intelligence, but I remembered what George had said about values and how they had to match. I felt sorry for them both. A while later, Kel was returning from the bathroom and paused at my bedroom door.

"Can I come in and talk to you?" she asked.

"Sure," I said and laid my book down on the comforter.

She sat down on the edge of the bed and hugged a pillow to her full tummy. "Donna, I read the bio, the answers to the questions on the agency form and saw all the pictures," she said, "but seeing you in person has really eased my mind. I've worried so much about the baby I'm going to have. And now that we've met, I'm really sure I've made the right decision. Actually, you're more like an aunt to me than someone I hardly knew until today. See, I was raised by my grandparents and was real close to my Aunt Pat. They were kind and loving people and we had a lot of good times together. I have some great memories of growing up in my grandparent's home and playing in their yard." Her eyes grew large and round as she glanced around the room. "Your house is gorgeous," she remarked. "The lake, the mountains, the small town atmosphere. It's a great place for a child to grow up. We could never give her this." Kel squeezed the pillow tighter to her and said, "I have a favor to ask. You don't have to say yes, but would you send pictures of Mariah a couple times a year? I would love to see how she's growing up."

"I wouldn't mind at all," I said. "What if I send pictures on her birthday and at Christmas?" Kel nodded and gave me a big smile. This time I was the one who picked up a pillow and hugged it. For my peace of mind and for the good of the birth parents, I felt it necessary to clarify before and after the adoption ground rules. "Kel, now I have a favor to ask of you and Connor."

"Okay. Fair enough," she replied.

"Until the time the baby is born, she's yours and you have the right to change your mind. Just pick up the phone, call collect and I'll honor your wish. But the moment I sign the papers, she becomes mine and there's no turning back. How do you feel about that, Kel?" I held my breath and waited for her response.

She gave my question some thought and said, "I feel okay. But, I think you're meant to be her mother. I — I already have a son and a daughter and I can't raise this child. I'm not married, don't have the money, the education — I'm a casino worker and Connor hasn't worked for a long time. He's living with another woman," Kel said in a flat voice. "We want to know the baby will be loved and raised in a nice home, and that she'll see and do things we could never afford. Connor wants her to have a good education. He got bored in school, but no one ever cared why. No one had him tested for IQ. And you know who raised me. There was no money for college. We both want the baby to have a parent that loves her and can make her feel wanted."

I grinned. It was what I wanted to hear. "Thank you, Kel, for believing in me. Do you want to know why I named her Mariah?" Kel nodded. "I had a wonderful vision. She actually came to me and told me her name."

"Wow. That's really cool. I like her name," Kel said, easing herself into a standing position. "I like it a lot."

I shed tears the next day after I put Kel, Connor and Mariah's sister on the flight back toLas Vegas. Tears of joy and elation. It was really happening. My daughter — coming to me at last. After I returned home, I got out the baby shower list and called my friends. Several of them subtly asked, "What if she changes her mind?"

I refused to allow that fear to enter my mind and replied, "My heart tells me Mariah is coming soon and I believe it."

Over the next few days, I completed reams of adoption papers. Just when I thought I'd filled everything out, another stack came in the mail. I had visited Mariah's room hundreds of times, making sure everything was ready and perfect, right down to pink blankets and disposable diapers.

Kel's caesarean section was scheduled for June twenty third. I would arrive in Las Vegas two days prior. I wanted to make sure I'd be at the hospital for the birth. I was so excited, I had insomnia that entire week. On the night of the twentieth, I received a phone call at six thirty. A woman's voice at the other end said, "I'm Kel's roommate, Donna. You are the proud mother of a healthy and beautiful nine-pound-four-ounce baby girl. She's 21 inches long and was born at 6:06 this evening."

I couldn't believe my ears. At first, I was speechless. All my planning and sleepless nights and Mariah had decided to enter the world in her own time. I recalled George saying "she's a pistol" and wondered if this was an indication of things yet to come. "Are you sure the baby is okay?" I asked when I'd recovered my voice.

"Just fine," I heard.

Questions raced through my mind. "Is the mother okay? Were there complications?"

"No," the roommate replied, "Kel — everyone is just fine."

"Why was the baby born so early?" I asked.

"Kel told me right after she talked to you this afternoon, her water broke and they took her straight to the hospital. Don't worry. There aren't any complications," the woman said.

I was hanging on every word. "Tell Kel I'm taking the first morning flight to Las Vegas and I'll come straight to the hospital. Then I remembered I had no idea where that was. "Oh — what's the name of the hospital?"

"Sunrise Hospital," the woman answered.

I was so excited, I could hardly think what to pack into my suitcase. I rushed around the house like a woman possessed, pulling out suitcases. Then, I dashed from room to room gathering diapers, plastic bottles, formula and toothbrush, curlers and cosmetics. I didn't take time to think how I would get it all on the plane. My mind kept clicking off items and I just kept tossing things into suitcases. Suddenly the reality hit. The magnitude of Kel giving birth had my nerves jumping like hot sparks. I plopped down on the floor amidst all the clutter and gathered myself together. Seventeen years ago when I had given up on life, I heard a voice say I would speak, write and have a daughter. And now, at last, my daughter was here. This was it! I was actually going to be a mom.

I remembered I hadn't called my mother with the news. I had decided to not say anything about the adoption to my mother until the papers were signed and I held my daughter in my arms. Now I wanted with all my heart to share my wonderful news and happiness with her. I would finally gain her approval, because, after all, I too was going to be a mother. I couldn't hold back my excitement as I dialed the phone.

My enthusiasm dwindled to the vanishing point when I heard, "Donna, you're too old to adopt a daughter. Now you'll never get a man. It takes time and money to raise a child on your own and you don't have either one. Why, you could lose your business and your house. It's ridiculous," she said and hung the phone up on me.

Her crushing words punched the air right out of me. Why couldn't she be pleased by the adoption? She was Mariah's grandmother — her only grandchild. I bit back tears as I dialed my brother. "Some one, please be happy for me," I said to myself.

Not having any children of his own, he was kind and seemed happy for me, but basically lukewarm about the news. By the time I called my father, I felt hollowed out inside and ready for anything. He didn't hang up on me and actually seemed pretty excited for me. I was surprised he was so supportive. By the time I called my step-father John at work, I felt a little more confidant. John was the only man I called Daddy and the one person who really understood me.

"Don't worry," he said. "Your mother will come around. She really wants the best for you. She's remembering how tough it was to raise you and your brother by herself. I think she just wants better for you." And then he gave me real encouragement. "Donna, you've always wanted a child. I think it's wonderful. It's your life and don't let anyone steal your dream."

"Thank you, Daddy," I said, "I won't." I knew John would work on my behalf to change my mother's thinking. John and I loved each other unconditionally. In fact, I was closer to him than my real father. My loving relationship with John had convinced me that love and not blood connects the souls. It's people who make the difference. Though Mariah wouldn't be biologically my child, she would always be mine.

The next morning, I took the first flight to Las Vegas and went right to the hospital. I found Kel in her room sitting up in bed, holding Mariah. I walked slowly toward the bed feeling an outpouring of love and intense emotion well up in my throat. For thirty years, I'd dreamed of this moment — of having a child. When Kel held the baby out to me, I took her in my arms and gazed down at the tiny, perfect creature of God. I was overcome with love. I held her like a fragile china doll and said, "She's beautiful, she's perfect, I love her."

Kel, observing my lack of experience holding the baby said, "Donna, relax, she's not going to break."

When Mariah let out a wail, my motherly instincts came alive, and I cooed and rocked her back to calmness like it was an every-day occurrence. I had such a strong sense of pride. The diaper was more difficult. Kel and I both laughed at my clumsiness when changing Mariah. Her tiny body seemed lost in the huge diaper.

"How many diapers have you changed?" Kel asked, eyeing my bumbling efforts.

"None," I replied, "but I'm a fast learner."

By Nevada law, custody of the child is granted the birth parents for seventy two hours.

They can then decide to keep the child or give it up. The social worker explicitly stated I could not have physical contact with Mariah unless Kel was present and handed me the child. Above all, I couldn't face losing my child and I made a point to follow the rules. But, I spent every moment I could in the hospital room with Kel and Mariah. The more I discovered about my daughter, the more endeared she became to me and the more impatient I was to bring her home.

Kel was alone with Mariah from seven in the morning until my visitation time at eleven o'clock. I literally danced from foot to foot until I was allowed in to the room. She had four hours every morning to bond with Mariah. I'd stand at the door watching Kel rocking Mariah, and murmuring sweet sounds to her daughter like any other new mother. I used every ounce of energy to center myself and to stay calm. A part of me worried that Kel might change her mind and not be able to give Mariah up, a lingering fear, relieved only when I cradled her in my arms again. When my visitation was up in the evening and I returned Mariah to Kel, the cold knot of uncertainty reappeared. I reminded myself to keep building plans for a lifetime around the child I adored.

Besides my apprehensions about Kel changing her mind, I also needed to know Connor's true feelings about the adoption. Until now he had stayed a shadow in the background. My opportunity to talk to him came while we were standing at the nursery window peering in at the babies. Mariah was sleeping peacefully in her bassinet, while some of the less healthy and premature infants were connected to tubes and machines. "It's a blessing Mariah is so beautiful and in such good health," I remarked.

Connor nodded and said, " You'll give her direction and keep her focused, Donna. Not like me. I was bored in school. I messed up. He turned to me and smiled. "I want Mariah to have a good education and learn some history."

I looked deep into his eyes and saw no hint of regret. "I promise to make sure that happens," I said.

As we walked away from the nursery, I said, "Connor, you have a beautiful daughter."

He said, "She was never meant to be my daughter. " He paused and studied me for a moment. "Isn't it weird how two strangers gave you what you wanted more than anything else?"

I smiled and said, "Maybe not so weird, but more like destiny. I'll love her, Connor."

At last, there were only hours left to wait. I called the agency in Nevada to make certain my social worker would be at the hospital for the signing of the adoption papers and was told she was on vacation and I would have to wait until Monday. I couldn't believe what I'd heard when they said Mariah could either go home with the parents for the week-end, or she would be placed in foster care.

Stress gushed though my body, my voice shook and I could barely croak out a response. "Th — that's not acceptable. The — the seventy two hours are almost up. I want my child. We have to sign the papers," I said with mounting panic. "Please, can't someone else come?" I was told to call back in an hour. Sixty minutes seemed like sixty hours, but I refused to be beaten down. The hunger to hold my daughter in my arms overpowered all else. I paced the hospital corridor wringing my hands, eyeballing the clock and praying for the minute hand to grow wings — angel wings. I was so overwrought, I couldn't bear to go into Kel's room to discuss it with her. The moment the minute hand hit the hour, I was on the phone with the agency.

"We have good news," they said. "We contacted your social worker at home. She's willing to come off her vacation and be at the hospital for the signing. She said she definitely wanted to be there."

I heaved a huge sigh and hung up the phone. As I walked down the corridor to Kel's room, I mentally thanked the social worker for her compassion. Before I entered Kel's room, I warmed up a big smile. She seemed especially uptight because Connor had left and hadn't returned. I assured her the social worker was on her way and would be at the hospital by six o'clock. I checked my watch. We still had a little time.

"That's great," Kel said. "I sure hope Connor will be here by then. I know he's with her," she said, sounding defeated.

However, when the social worker and the notary arrived, there was still no sign of Connor. I thanked them both for giving up their time and was told it would take about two hours to get through the stack of paper work. Kel kept fidgeting and watching the clock. He was late and we were all on edge.

By the time Connor arrived, it was obvious Kel was furious. The air in the room was thick with tension. The social worker had picked up on the antagonism and asked me to wait outside in the hall while she talked to them. I glanced over at Kel and Connor, a pleading look in my eyes that signaled, "please don't change your mind." I was so close that even a delay of one second was unbearable.

I leaned back against the wall in the corridor, on pins and needles. What if Kel and Connor decided to change their minds? What would I do? How could I get through the disappointment? What advice would George give me now? As soon as I asked the question, the answer came.

> "Keep your mind on the target.
> Center your energy and trust the
> Universe will provide for you."

Thank you, George. "Mariah is coming to me," I told myself. "It will happen." I folded my arms tight over my chest and rocked to the sound of her name playing in my mind.

The social worker came out of the room. "It's settled," she said smiling. "It had nothing to do with you, Donna. They were fighting over Connor being late because he was with the new girlfriend. We can proceed. You and Kel go down to the nursery and get Mariah while I read Connor his birth father rights. After that, you can bring the baby into the room."

I'd held my breath the entire time the social worker talked. Her reassuring words left me gasping out my thanks.

Together, Kel and I walked to the nursery. For me, walking on eggshells was an understatement. I watched her sign Mariah out and we began wheeling her down the hall back to the room. The two of us were much calmer as we chatted about baby stuff and how anxious I was to introduce Mariah to Sheba. Kel suddenly stopped talking and lifted her head. Panic crept over her face. A sharp blade of fear knifed through me. There wasn't much time left and she still had a right to change her mind. I clutched my stomach and gripped the bassinet to steady myself. I couldn't fall apart now. I swallowed hard and blurted out, "Kel, what is it? What's wrong?"

"I smell smoke," she said, becoming even more agitated. "No one is allowed to smoke in the nursery area." She darted from room to room searching out the offensive odor. When she returned, she said, "I don't understand. No one is smoking, but I can still smell it. It smells weird — like cherry."

I gasped. It was beyond my wildest dreams. I paused to sniff the air and smelled the familiar aroma of cherry tobacco.

"You're here, George," I said aloud. "Just like you promised." Tears of joy welled up and ran down my cheeks. I glanced down at Mariah, then smiled at Kel and said, "I don't know whether you believe in these things, but my dear friend, George, promised me he'd be here when I got my daughter. I was heartbroken when he passed away last year. I wanted him to be here. He was a huge part of my life and I still miss him so much."

"I was the first one to smell it, Donna," Kel declared. She shook her head bewildered. "I really don't believe in this stuff, but I know he's here. How can that be?"

I scanned the hall, as if expecting him to appear momentarily and said. "George always said life is eternal, that he'd always watch over me and be with me."

Kel nodded. "I guess he's still a big part of you." She turned her gaze on me. "I — I need to tell you something, Donna."

My heart skipped a beat. *Please — don't change your mind.* "Sure," I said, scarcely able to look at her.

"Do you know why I really chose you, a single mom in her forties, to be Mariah's adopted mother?" Kel asked.

"No," I said, feeling my racing heart slow, "but, I'd like to know."

Kel looked down at Mariah sleeping in the bassinet. "Don't ask me why, but I know she's going to be a leader. You can make that happen. I'm so busy working and looking after kids, I can't even keep up with what's going on in the world. And I do know how much you love her. Why, you have more energy at your age than I have. You'll make a great mom. The bond between the two of you is wonderful to see." Kel sighed and said, "I hope someday I can be a happy person like you. And you're kind and thought-ful. I doubt anyone else would offer to keep Connor and me up-to-date about Mariah's progress and to send us pictures."

I hugged Kel and said, "Thank you for believing in me. And you know what? In the plane crash, a voice came to me and said I would have a daughter late in life who would be a leader. Even George said that."

I glanced down at Mariah, peaceful in the bassinet and murmured, "Someday, I'll tell you all about George, my wise man and my mentor, but today, I truly believe he is my angel."

I wheeled Mariah into the hospital room for the last milestone. Connor was painstakingly meticulous about reading all the fine print on the stack of documents. Holding Mariah in my arms helped, but I was frazzled. Each time the social worker explained that Connor and Kel had the right to change their mind, my heart flip-flopped. I kept telling myself, "It won't be long until she's mine."

When the process was over, tears of joy welled up and ran down my cheeks. I was deliriously happy. "You've made the right decision, Kel — Connor," I said softly. And with Mariah in my arms, I walked from the room.

Mariah and I took a taxi back to the motel. I was pretty confident, until then. I'd read all the right books on baby care and had bought the prescribed formula and the safest car seat. Everything I would need. And still my imagination went into overtime. What if the formula disagreed with Mariah? What do I do when she cries? How many times was I supposed to change her diaper? Would something awful happen if she didn't burp? What if the hic-ups didn't go away? I had four baby outfits with me and couldn't even decide which one to dress her in. I got very little sleep that night. I kept hopping out of bed to check if Mariah was still breathing — and to see if she was wet.

The next morning I realized I'd brought way too much "baby stuff." I had called a taxi to take us to the airport and it was waiting outside the motel. With Mariah in my arms, I made trip after trip to the elevator — car seat, suitcases, diaper bag and formula. When the doors slid open, I used my foot to keep them from closing. Balancing Mariah on my one free shoulder, I used my butt, my other foot, anything to stuff our belongings inside. After we reached the lobby, I pulled everything out of the elevator and piece by piece, took the baggage outside to the waiting taxi. I almost lost it when I had to tangle with the car seat. By the time I figured it out and got Mariah strapped up, I was drenched in sweat.

When we reached the airport, I thanked the Universe for the kindness of strangers. My luggage was looked after by a pleasant father of six, a pilot held Mariah while I rummaged in my purse for my ticket. I totally forgot about the pull down changing stations in the restroom. I ignored the stares from people around me in the waiting area and somehow got her diaper changed. I dismissed the idea of having a cup of tea or something to eat because where was I to put the baby? My nerves were shot and I was on the verge of tears — a mother of a four-day-old infant and completely unequipped to cope.

I'd made many friends teaching seminars at the airlines and they promised me an upgrade to first class when I brought Mariah home. I was elated until I observed the glares from the other passengers. I thought, where was the sign that said I couldn't bring a baby into first class? Even the flight attendant treated me like an outcast. I was worried Mariah would cry, but I couldn't have asked for a more well-behaved baby. She slept through the entire flight.

After we landed and I stood to leave, a woman passenger said, "Your baby was very good. I thought for sure she'd be fussy."

"Thank you," I said. "She's just four days old. I'm so excited to bring her home. I've wanted a child for thirty years. I've been trying to adopt for seven years and I finally have my baby." The woman looked shocked. After that, she and her husband fell over themselves to help me.

I left our luggage with a sky cap and I carried Mariah to the car. Then I remembered the trip home would take a full hour, so

I fed Mariah a bottle before we left the airport. During the drive to Tahoe, I worried over the tremendous responsibility I had undertaken — raising a child by myself. Could I take care of her when she got sick? Would I make her happy? How much should I set aside for her college fund? The questions piled up faster than I could answer them.

I brought Mariah into the new home I had equipped for her and laid her on the sofa. For several minutes, I stared down at her in disbelief, as if I were frozen to the spot. Then I started to cry, the tears rolling down my cheeks. I kept blubbering, "She's here. She's beautiful. After all this time — I'm finally a mom. I can't believe it. Thank you, God. Thank you." I was deliriously happy, and yet I bordered on hysteria. Thirty years of pain and disappointment had ended with a dream answered. Now at last, I could hold her, hug her. She was real.

I pulled myself together, gathered up Mariah and walked to the bedroom. I gently laid her on my bed. Sheba's feline vibrations had already sensed something was about to take place. She hopped up with a soft thud and sniffed the baby. I said, "Sheba, meet your sister, Mariah." I had imagined this would be a rather significant moment, instead her brilliant blues seemed to say, "Okay, so she's here — just don't forget about me." Then, she curled up at the bottom of the bed and went to sleep. I tucked Mariah into the bassinet and withdrew my Journal from the nightstand drawer.

It was awhile before I could sort through the past events and actually write about what I had learned. How could I describe in words the blissful happiness and overwhelming love I was experiencing. People had warned me about the work involved in raising a child, but no one had mentioned the intimacy and love that bonds mother and child together. I suddenly felt George's presence, powerful and certain, as if he were standing before me. I felt relieved and had an immense need to talk to him. I sat down on the edge of the bed and said, "George, you were so right when you said I'd be a mom. All those years I begged and pleaded with you finally paid off. She's really here and just like you said, she's a pistol. George, thank you, I love you and please watch over us.

JOURNAL
Center Your Energy

I have learned to trust my intuition. I didn't doubt when I had the vision of a baby girl who said she was coming to me. I bought baby furniture, prepared her bedroom and made a baby shower list. I now understand what George meant when he said to be aware of my energy. When I took action, my dream came true. I didn't just sit and do nothing and expect it to fall in my lap. The Universe expects me to do my work. I overcame the negative thinking and other people's disapproval, and I didn't loose sight of my purpose. Neither my age or being single held me back from adopting a child. George said,

> "Energy comes from within. Obstacles become learning lessons and it's the lessons that move you forward."

And there is no question in my mind that the soul never dies. It continues on. Georgeproved that when his mystical self and cherry pipe tobacco appeared at the hospital. He had promised to be there and he was. The wisdom George has bestowed on me for so many years is beginning to surface. *I have learned to ask for spiritual help when I need it and to trust my higher self.* I want to make him proud of his student because he was and is a master teacher. *I miss you, George.*

I understand there is no magic formula for gaining inner calmness and peace. I'll need to work hard, but I need this for me and for my daughter. I don't want to pass on negative patterns or confusion. I claim for myself to center my energy and thereby clear all blocks and advance toward integrity and truth.

> **I center my energy to
> be a student of life.**

The Gift of
Inner Peace

The Christmas season had officially arrived in Tahoe. Crisp, unseasonably warm air whispered through the glistening pine forest. Snow capped peaks floated on the cloudless skyline above the dazzling blue lake. I was enjoying a leisurely drive home from town with Mariah. She was fast asleep in the back of the car after a stroller ride to see the Christmas lights and a trip to the grocery store.

This was my favorite time of year and although some people were at their most miserable during Christmas, I was at my happiest. Approaching the beginning of a new year gave me time to reflect on the past year, my accomplishments and challenging learning lessons; to count my blessings; and to prepare and look forward to exciting changes and the wonderful promise in the days ahead. It was a time of peace and relaxation and a time to cut back travel and busy schedules. What I didn't like was the commercialism and the pressure of buying gifts. Adults and children alike got swept up in buying gifts, and the holiday festivities and meaningful time with loved ones went by the wayside.

My daughter had just turned six months old and I couldn't believe she was actually starting to resemble me. I'd come a long way since those first weeks of insecurity. I had learned to juggle my purse, bags of groceries and had actually mastered the car seat. George had always stressed the importance of balance in my life. I just never anticipated it meant sleepless nights and coordinating my work schedule with making formula and feeding times. Still, without a doubt, Mariah was the joy of my life.

When I ended up in the local emergency ward, diagnosed as suffering from exhaustion, I wondered if every conscious mother felt pulled in a hundred different directions. Or did I just over-compensate because I wanted to be superwoman? There were still moments when I questioned my decision to raise a daughter without a father. How would I answer when Mariah asked why she didn't have a daddy? And, could I manage a business, a house-hold and raise a daughter by myself? I searched for answers only time could give. A stable environment was important to Mariah's well-being and I didn't want to bungle raising my child. She required set routines, the newness of change and simple pleasures, but mostly, she needed all the love I could give her every day.

I glanced over my shoulder at my sleeping daughter zipped up to the neck in her warm sleeper and my aunt's hand knitted blanket tucked around her. I had cut back my speaking engagements and altered my lifestyle. Spending time with my child was more important than manicures, pedicures and a new outfit.

I pulled into my driveway to the welcome sight of my home decked out in brilliant outdoor lights and my crimson and silver tree glowing in the widow. My mother had faithfully sent new decorations every year and I had always done Christmas to the max. She never missed the after-Christmas sales in our hometown of Bethlehem, Pennsylvania and always sent a box of exquisite new holiday decorations. I had accumulated so many ornaments that the tree's green branches seemed lost in a brilliant web of gingerbread men, miniature Santas, red velvet bows and jeweled garlands. She still wasn't speaking to me since the adoption and I would have given anything just to hear the sound of her voice. I wanted to put the phone to Mariah's ear so she could hear Nana on the other end. Nowadays I wondered when, if ever, that would happen.

Mariah was still asleep in the warm car and I decided to leave her be while I unloaded the groceries. Sheba was waiting at the door and gave me one of those looks that said, "Where's what's her name?" She pretty much kept her distance from the baby. I placated her by saying Mariah was in the car and I had brought home lots of great cat food.

After I put the groceries away, I went out to the car to collect my daughter. I stopped dead in my tracks when I looked into the back seat. Sheba, who up until now just "tolerated" the kid, and acted like the house was still her private domain, had jumped through the open window and was curled up in the back seat beside Mariah, purring contentedly.

I had waited years to be swept up in all the wonderful emotions of this special moment. I knew at last, I had a family. Maybe not the traditional kind, but for the first time, two little souls that adored me. I smiled to myself and said, "Yes, George, I've made a good choice. I have the right family for me. I will never question if love is enough again."

I was laughing as I hoisted Mariah over one shoulder and Sheba over the other. When I went inside, I was still smiling over my little family. I warmed a bottle in the microwave and sat down on the sofa to feed Mariah. Sheba jumped up and got comfortable beside us. When I looked down at them, I thought how beautiful they were and experienced the pride and closeness of family. My decision to adopt was a right and powerful one. I had changed the course of our lives.

I laid Mariah down on her blanket to play and watched her eyes grow wide and her face, beneath the tree lights, glow with happiness. I built a fire in the fireplace and lit aromatic candles scented with pine and clove. As I glanced around the room at my child, my cat and the gifts under the tree waiting to be opened, the true meaning of Christmas flooded my thoughts: a time to give thanks to God, to recount all the lessons learned, to plan for the new year and to reflect on good friends and loved ones. I was so blessed and I just knew Mariah's first Christmas would be my best Christmas ever.

It saddened me to know my mother and I wouldn't share the holidays together. But, she had sent a check for Mariah and a box of gifts that had sat beneath the tree for weeks. I stooped down and reached under the tree for her package. Then, I tenderly removed the wrappings and opened it. Inside were little outfits and a variety of stuffed animals for Mariah. I clutched one of the animals to my heart and prayed my mother's thoughtfulness was a sign she might be accepting Mariah as her granddaughter. I wanted desperately to talk with her and even tried to imagine what I would say. I yearned to share with her a lifetime of Mariah moments — as an infant, a toddler and as a young lady. I had to keep trying. Somehow I had to reach her. I clutched the phone in my hand wavering between the hope that we would speak and the reasons behind why I should not set myself up to be hurt again — then I dialed my mother's number in Bethlehem.

I heard several rings before my stepdad, John, answered. "Hi, Daddy," I said, fraught with hope, "I called to wish you and Mom a Merry Christmas."

"And to you too, Donna. Merry Christmas. Your mother isn't home," he said, sadness obvious in his voice.

My body sagged with disappointment. "Okay, Daddy," I said, feeling the sting of tears. "Please thank her for the beautiful gifts she sent Mariah. The clothes are the perfect size and all the right colors and — would you please have her call me?"

"I'll give her your message, Honey. How's the *new* mom?" John asked. Getting any sleep yet?"

"Some. Never enough, Daddy, but I still love being a mom."

"I can hear it in your voice, Donna," he said. "Now, don't worry about your mother. I'm working on her all the time and she'll come around. I think she's accepted Mariah. She just has an issue about you being an older mother. But, you put that aside and have a wonderful first Christmas with your daughter."

"Thank you, Daddy. I love you." I understood how my mother didn't want me to experience the difficulties of raising a child on my own, but the real reasons for our falling out were because she thought I was too old, didn't have enough money, and now that I had a child, would never get a man. After months of her rejection, I had come to a decision. Somehow, I'd make my mother understand I was no longer a child, that I was an adult capable of making intelligent decisions and that Mariah was an absolute major part of my life.

When the phone rang, I was so startled, I almost knocked over the lamp reaching for it. The call came in on my private line and I instantly thought, my mother. It turned out to be a close girlfriend. I did a bad job hiding my disappointment.

"You sound so let down," she said.

I apologized and said, "I'm really glad to hear from you, I just thought it was my mother calling me back."

We chatted for awhile about my friend's family. When I hung up the phone I started thinking about my own family. My brother hadn't visited Mariah and me, but he had, on occasion, called to ask how we were. I felt sad we had drifted apart, because as kids we were inseparable. I wanted that closeness again. I called him and after a typical conversation pleaded, "Let's get together soon." The heaviness around my heart lifted after he promised to come up and ski, and to spend time with Mariah and me.

On the other hand, my father had made a point to visit several times. He brought Mariah a high chair and a portable heater for her bedroom. In his own way, he tried, but the deep bonding so necessary to form a loving family relationship was still on my hopeful list.

Mariah was a healthy child and growing tall and physically strong, but my concern was her mental development. At day's end, before I tucked her in, I developed a ritual to help stimulate her mind. I stroked her back, talked to her, played lullabies and afterwards, I always placed six positive thoughts in her memory. There were times I'd say, "You're beautiful, you're healthy, you're happy, you're a wise soul, I love you and God loves you." I had learned from George, Catharina and Raimund that affirmative words affect the mind in a positive way and I figured spending a few extra minutes before bed could prevent Mariah from spending thousands of dollars in therapy. I truly believed if someone had planted positive statements in my mind at a young age, my mind and body would have worked in harmony and the obstacles blocking my path would not have been boulders, but mere obstacles. These end-of-the-day moments invoked the growth of higher self for Mariah and me.

Though George could no longer give me conventional information, my unanswered questions about Mariah seemed to create answers on their own. It took seventeen years after the plane crash to believe my daughter was coming. I was given that message in the crash, and yet I kept asking "when is she coming and where will I find her — and why so long a wait? Is it that she isn't ready to come to me — or that I'm not ready for the responsibility of motherhood? Do I have too much baggage to clean up — or too many negative patterns from the past?" Since I had jumped from one self-destructive pattern to another, maybe deep down a part of me believed I didn't really deserve her. Today it's clear that I wasn't ready. Mariah came at the right time, when I had learned my lessons about life from George. Thinking back, I distinctly remember him saying:

> "Two souls come together
> when the time is right
> for both of them."

I smiled and glanced up at his picture on the mantel. The day was still vivid in my mind. George with his pipe in hand strolling along the path surrounded by trees and nature's creatures. He had lectured me hard that day and now I understand why. He died soon after. I'm sure he's up there looking down on me — laughing at my fumbling and bumbling, my silly panic over Mariah's hiccups and crying spells, my overanxious phone calls to the pediatrician. "But, I'm doing it, George, and I'm learning what it means to be a good mother." I giggled, thinking if anyone heard me talking to George, they'd haul me off to the looney bin. I looked up and down and all around the room thinking he could be anywhere and everywhere. But then I decided there was nothing wrong with having a chat with an old friend — nothing wrong with talking to an old soul. . .

George, I remember the conversations we had after the crash, when I told you I kept waking up at night feeling scared because I felt someone was there. You smiled at me and said how blessed I was to be getting enlightenment from the other side and that two guides were with me at night. You said they were there to help me clean up the obstructions holding me back from understanding what a real life called for, that my vulnerable state and being at rest enabled them to contact me. After that, when I sensed they were near me, I relaxed and asked them to help me.

After a while, they disappeared and I actually felt sad. You said, "Don't worry, Donna, and don't be sad, you learned what they had to teach you and they moved on."

George, this time it's your presence I feel. Please, give me your guidance. I don't want my daughter to get caught up in the material stuff, the neediness and the to-do list like I did. I want her to have the wisdom not to be controlled by the outside, but to make choices guided by her inner vision. Time and again you drilled into me,

"When who you are on the inside is who you are on the outside, you'll find inner vision and become the person you were destined to be. Obstacles aren't setbacks, they're lessons."

Then you would take off on one your parables. Back then, I got sick and tired of listening to all the stories. Today, I think about their enlightening messages all the time. I've grown from your stories and the more I grow, the better mom I'll be, the better speaker, the better person.

At last, I understand how to get very clear and ask if it's for my highest good. It's taken me my entire life to grasp that I cannot force what's meant to be a natural flow. Because I didn't understand, I forced a lot of situations and a lot of men. No more, George. You can't force love.

This seems to be the right time of year to tell you again how grateful I am to you for always being there for me. Even though you're an angel, you're still my number one mentor. I miss your lectures and the smell of your tobacco. I miss knowing you're only a phone call away when I need you. I'll remember you in my heart as the kindest, dearest friend I've ever had. And I promise to do what you asked — pass on your wisdom to other people.

Thank you for keeping your word and for being there when I got my daughter. She's great and she is a pistol, just like you said. Her green eyes are so clear — like yours. I'm just beginning a wonderful journey with her. You said I would learn to listen to my knowing. And I know, *the soul never dies*. George, would you hear my SOS from time to time and help me out? I bugged you down here. I might as well bug you up there. Like now. I want to heal with my mother and father and it seems that path is blocked. Is there another way? I love them. Isn't that enough? Mariah needs grandparents and whether they know it or not, they need her.

Remember I said if I had a choice, I would never have chosen my parents. It was so painful growing up with them. You stood solid as old ironsides and wouldn't budge on this issue. You said,

"Donna, you chose your parents before you were born. They made you who you are today and they pass on the lessons you're destined to learn. Doesn't matter when you learn the lessons — this week, or this year — or if it takes a lifetime. The chance is given to you by your parents and the choice is yours. Thank your parents for the challenges they have given you. You will stop the patterns in your family and raise your daughter the way you want to raise her — with incredible love and laughter."

George, I don't want to pass my baggage on to her — and not to generation after generation. It has to stop with me, now.

I stood and crossed the room to the window. The night was clear and the starry sky shimmered down on the fresh snow blanketing the ground. Unburdening myself to George got me thinking of the wisdom communicated to me from all the mentors who had crossed my life. People like Raimund, my ski guide. Actually, more than just a ski guide — an advisor on life, love, relationships and the significance of self-respect — an insightful man with a kind heart. I remember his words, *"Live in the moment. Don't be afraid to go for it."* And Catherina, the laughing saint. *"Take charge of your life from the inside out,"* she'd say. *"Be, just be."* Like George used to say, *"Life is pretty simple. It's man that complicates it."*

Tonight and every night, I thank my mentors for teaching me from their hearts, for their kindness and sternness, for their insight and inner wisdom — and for being angels. I won't forget those of you who weren't my mentors, who were my learning lessons and my pain. You also had a purpose in my life. You gave me awareness the hard way, through pain, suffering and tears. I will not attract those lessons to me again.

I've come a long way since I was queen of pots and pans. Selling cookware was the real motivator behind my increased self-confidence and winning the title of Miss Hawaii after five tries. Chuck, my relentless boss, taught me to manage money, time, a crew of people and encouraged me to put myself through college. I smiled, thinking back to when he'd complain because he couldn't reach me on the phone. He knew all along I was surfing.

My accountant said I should write a book on how I live on attitude because I sure don't live on cash. He was right. I'm not wealthy from a financial standpoint, but I have abundance in my life. Spiritual abundance — a gift created in our belief system.

> **God provides for all and gives us abundance. We are all God.**

I glanced down at Mariah kicking her tiny feet beneath the tree, cooing at the lights and shiny ornaments. So contented. Except for the crackle of logs burning in the fireplace, the house was wrapped in silence. I looked out the window up at the sky and said, "George, I'm ready. I want to heal my life on all levels and create my destiny."

I knew with every ounce of my being he'd be nearby helping me. This was a most unusual night, an inspiring night filled with hope. As I headed for the kitchen to put the kettle on for tea, I suddenly had a wonderful desire to hear Christmas music. It was my little girl's first Christmas and why shouldn't we get into the holiday spirit? I moved to the bookshelves and began searching out the labels on my CD's.

I soon realized I had placed the Christmas music to the back of the shelf. I rummaged around and found a Christmas CD and much to my surprise, one of my *30 Days to Success* books tucked away with the music. I gazed tenderly at the book, remembering the last time George and I had talked before he died. I knew instantly it was the very same book he had read and returned to me in the Denver airport.

"This is going to be a winner for you. It's good stuff," he said, "and it'll help a lot of people. When you get home, put this copy in a safe place for luck."

I'd done exactly that. I thumbed through the pages, unaware of anything except my own nostalgia, until a single sheet of folded paper fell from the book and fluttered to the floor. I bent down, picked it up and slowly unfolded it.

George's handwriting was scrawled across a page of his stationary. For a moment, I stared unseeing at the paper in my hand. The thought crossed my mind he might have used it to mark a page and had forgotten to take it out. I felt it might be something I had no business reading. Then, I remembered him saying,

> "There are no accidents. Everything happens for a reason. Once you understand your learning lessons, you'll achieve inner widsom."

That day, while we waited in the airport, he said to keep the book in a safe place. I now realized he intended for me to find it. I sat down in the overstuffed chair, turned on the light and began to read:

Hi Partner —

If you are reading this now, the time is right. When I came across this message, I knew it would someday give you the inner vision to create change in ways you thought impossible. That time is now:

Do not stand at my grave and weep:
I am not there, I do not sleep.
I am a thousand winds that blow,
I am the diamond glints on snow.
I am the sunlight on ripened grain,
I am the gentle autumn's rain.
When you awaken in the morning's hush,
I am the swift uplifting rush
Of quiet birds in circled flight.
I am the soft stars that shine at night...
Do not stand at my grave and cry...
I am not there, I did not die.

I sat in the quiet room reading George's message over and over, swiping at tears rolling down my cheeks. I imagined George sitting wherever he might be at this moment, a knowing smile lighting up his clear eyes and pipe smoke curling all around him. An ancient soul — a man who practiced the truth of the ages and passed his wisdom on to others in very simplistic ways. His sound guidance and passion for the truth are permanently stamped on my memory. And I can hear him today, like he was standing next to me,

> "Keep it simple and keep it truthful.
> Let your inner vision be your guide
> to the truth inside of you:
> ask, listen, trust and act. If you do
> the steps, the inner vision follows."

I finally understand the meaning of inner vision: to know what is right for me and to act on that decision. When I think back to the chapters in my life, I can truly appreciate the reasons behind the lessons George taught me. He was guiding me, step by step, down the path to *self love and acceptance*. He taught me to *focus on values* and why they were important to me. He was insistent that I act *for my highest good*, that we are *blessed with mentors* who can help us along our path if we just listen. He instilled in me the importance of undertaking the smallest task with *passion*. And I have to laugh when I think of how insightful George was about my house and how he taught me *action creates attraction*. He advised me to *trust my intuition* because all the answers are inside of me, that once I *centered my energy*, I could create and manifest. He was right because Mariah came to me. The most precious gift

George ever gave me were the steps to *tap into my inner vision:* ask, listen, trust and act.

Sheba broke my concentration by pawing ornaments, and decorative bows on the tree. When she tired of that, she curled up next to Mariah. I wiped away the last of my tears and said, "How about I turn on some Christmas music, pour some eggnog and I'll play with you? I glanced down at George's message on the table next to my chair, at my beautiful child and cat and understood beyond all doubt, the significance of being blessed with abundant love and peace. Then I asked myself the four questions:

> Do you love yourself?...
> Do you have a good relationship
> with your family and friends?...
> Are you living your goals and dreams?...
> If you die today, have you left this
> planet a better place for being here?

For the first time, I answered a definite "yes" to the most meaningful gift I could ever give to myself and others. "Merry Christmas, Mariah and Sheba and — Merry Christmas, George."

> **Open your life to
> inner vision**

Epilogue

A child's first birthday calls for a celebration. The guests would soon be arriving, the mouth watering chocolate cake with a single candle was begging to be eaten, and Mariah's presents were wrapped in gilded paper and tempting puffy bows. The telephone had rung continually the entire day and it was jangling again, urging someone to run and answer it. That someone was me. "Hello," I said catching my breath.

"Donna — it's Mother. I'm calling to wish Mariah a happy birthday and to ask if she received her gifts."

I was shocked to silence and took what seemed countless seconds to recover. "Uh — Mother — hello — the gifts, they're beautiful — thank you — and for calling." My heart pounded so hard, my ears rang.

"And I just wanted you to know," my mother went on as if this was a typical mother, daughter conversation, "Daddy John is having his seventieth birthday soon and we're giving him a party." A pause. "The only thing he wants for his birthday is to see you and his granddaughter. Will you and Mariah come?"

I swallowed hard and said, "Mom, thank you. We'll both be there.

> **Let the healing begin.**

About the Author

As so often happens, Donna Hartley started off down one road and ended up traveling on another. An aspiring actress in Hawaii, she thought winning the title of Miss Hawaii would give her career a much-needed boost. She won the title on her fifth try.

She moved to Los Angeles where she made enough to survive selling motor homes and boats, but still her acting career was going nowhere. She was desperate for a change.

It wasn't until the accident on Continental Airlines that change occurred. Although she escaped largely unharmed, something emerged in her spirit that allowed her to turn around and head in a positive direction. She began by crusading for airline safety, but as she did so a new career as motivational speaker took shape. She moved to Lake Tahoe, bought some business cards, and got busy in her new line of work.

It was a struggle at first; however, by the second year her personal income had more than doubled. Her work now concentrated on providing seminars and talks about customer service and organizational change for clients like Red Lion Hotels, Lockheed Martin and *New Woman* magazine.

But something was still missing. She realized she still hadn't attained the two things she'd always wanted more than aything else: a house and a baby. She soon found the house—with 2,800 square feet on Lake Tahoe—but the baby took a while longer. After searching agencies for eight years, she adopted her daughter, Mariah.

Today Donna is a member of the National Speakers Association and founder and owner of Hartley International. She hosted her own television show, "Get What You Want" and produced the series, "Everyday Heroes." With over 100 appearances on television, she also appeared on NBC, ABC, PBS, and the Learning Channel. She was also featured in *New Woman Magazine*, *The New York Times* and the best selling *Chocolate for a Woman's Soul* and *Chocolate for a Woman's Heart*. A master at weaving a story and a catalyst, she inspires positive change. Her revised thinking is a welcome antidote for today's "new ways."

VISIONS...

1. Love and Accept Yourself
2. Focus on Values
3. For My Highest Good
4. The Power of Mentors
5. Manifest Your Passion
6. Action Creates Attraction
7. Trust Your Intuition
8. Center Your Energy
9. The Gift of Inner Vision